Verena Kast

A TIME TO MOURN
Growing through the Grief Process

(Bibliography)

Verena Kast

A Time to Mourn
Growing through the Grief Process

DAIMON
VERLAG

Title of the original German edition:
Trauern: Phasen und Chancen des psychischen Prozesses,
by Verena Kast;
© 1982 Kreuz Verlag, Stuttgart
and Dieter Breitsohl AG, Literary Agency, Zürich.

A Time to Mourn: Growing through the Grief Process,
by Verena Kast;
translated from the German by Diana Dachler and Fiona Cairns.
Photo of Verena Kast © by Barbara Davatz.

First edition
copyright © 1988 by Daimon Verlag,
Am Klosterplatz, CH-8840 Einsiedeln, Switzerland

ISBN 3-85630-509-2

Printed in the United States of America

CONTENTS

FOREWORD

This book, originally published in 1982 in German, was translated without alteration into English in 1988. The original character of the book has been preserved although a great many additional thoughts on the subject of mourning have occurred to me over the years. A supplementary text dealing with the nature of relationships and related processes associated with separation has already appeared in English in *The Nature of Loving: Patterns of Human Relationship* (Chiron Publications, Wilmette, Illinois, 1986), and a further investigation into the distinction between depressive reactions and reactions of grief is in progress.

This investigation into the significance of mourning in the therapeutic process became a matter of pressing importance for me through my practical work as a psychotherapist. In the course of the last ten years, it again and again struck me in the treatment of many depressive illnesses that loss experiences had been too little mourned. It seemed clear that they could be an additional factor contributing to depressive illness.

The taboo surrounding death has been lifted in recent years. It is now 'permissible' to speak of dying. It seems to me that the time has come to also lift the taboo surrounding mourning: we may and we should mourn. Indeed, Freud wrote as early as 1915 about the great value of the "work of mourning" – the term originates from him. Nevertheless, the great influence which grief has on our psychic health is not in proportion to the rather scant attention paid to it in the literature of psychology.

For a period of ten years, I gathered material on this

subject, dream material in particular; on the basis of this material, I will try to illustrate systematically the way in which the unconscious prompts us to deal with mourning. I have set out my own observations in relationship to the results described in the more recent literature.

The following factors were of the greatest importance in my investigations:

– Because we perceive ourselves in a fundamental way in terms of relationships to others and because bonds are an essential part of the way we perceive ourselves and the world, these perceptions will be severely shaken by the death of a loved one. Grief is the emotion through which we take leave and deal with problems in the now collapsed relationship. Through mourning we can integrate as much as possible of this relationship and the partner in ourselves in order to be able to go on living with a new self-perception and in a new relationship to the world.

– From our dreams we receive valuable guidance in the task of mourning, which I try to illustrate by means of a dream series. Consideration of current literature on the phases of mourning has led me to make some modifications in my own point of view.

– Each of the phases of mourning presents special difficulties to be surmounted. Using practical examples from my therapeutic work, I shed some light on these difficulties.

– The need to linger in a symbiosis stands in opposition to the need to separate. In extreme cases this longing causes a long-term fusion with the deceased. I propose the hypothesis that the rhythm of symbiosis and individuation is essential not only for the small child, but for the adult as well. It seems to me to be important that the symbiosis between individuals is succeeded by a relationship to something transcendent.

– The death of a loved one is an extreme experience of death which requires radical mourning. At the same time, this event is an enormous challenge to the individual to develop his own potential when confronted with change.

8

Mourning can lead to greater self-realization. What is true in this extreme situation might also hold true, though in a less radical form, in many other human situations – situations in which it will be seen that death is always present in our lives, again and again demanding greater or lesser changes coupled with feelings of loss which therefore must also be mourned. Because we are mortal, we must exist in the "readiness to take leave." We are bound to sadness and pain and to the possibility of having to repeatedly rebuild our lives and also to unfold new potential as individuals as a result of the many leave-takings. In this respect, mourning is indispensable.

I would like at this point to thank all my analysands who have permitted me to use and publish their material.

My thanks go also to Robert Hinshaw, who made this book available to readers in the English language, and to Diana Dachler and Fiona Cairns who translated the book with competence and empathy.

Verena Kast

WHEN A LOVED ONE DIES

When a loved one dies, we *experience* what death is. The experience of death affects us deeply, disrupts our lives, and fills us with doubts not only regarding ourselves, but with respect to everything that we have until now taken for granted. It not only disturbs the way we perceive ourselves and the world, it compels us to change, whether we want to or not.

When a loved one dies, we not only experience our own deaths in an anticipatory way through this event; in a certain sense, we also die with him. At no other time are we made so sharply aware of the extent to which we understand and experience ourselves in terms of our relationships to others, and to what extent the loss of such a relationship tears us apart and demands of us a new orientation.

It is an experience as old as mankind itself. Among the many witnesses to this was the young St. Augustine, who had experienced the death of a friend.[1]

"Through this pain, a deep darkness came over my heart, and wherever I looked, there was death. The city I called home became a torment for me, the house of my father a place of rare unhappiness, and each and every thing that I had shared with him became for me now, without him, a source of unending pain. Everywhere my eyes searched for him, and he was not there. I hated everything, because he was no longer a part of it, and it could no longer say to me: 'See, he comes,' – as it had been when he still lived, when he was only absent. I became a single great question, and I searched in my soul to know why it

11

was so sad, why it so confused me, but my soul knew not how to answer. And when I said to it: Have faith in God, it did not obey, and it was right not to, because this friend, whom it counted as most precious and had lost, was better and truer than the illusion that I held out to it as hope. Only weeping was still sweet to me and among the joys of my heart took the place of my friend.

Within me ... an emotion of the most contradictory nature came to life – I don't know what it was: a complete weariness with life side by side with a fear of death. I believe that the more I loved him, the more I hated and feared death, which stole him from me like the grimmest of enemies, and I imagined death would suddenly devour everyone, because it had been able to devour him ... It surprised me, in other words, that the remaining mortals continued to live while he whom I loved so much had died, as if he might not have had to die, and even more I wondered at the fact that I, as his other ego, survived his death. Someone once called his friend the half of his soul (Horace, Od. 1.3): For I have felt mine and his soul as one in two bodies (reference to Ovid, Trict. IV, 4, 72), and for this reason I shuddered in the face of life, because I did not want to live as half a man; and for this reason I was afraid to die, because he, whom I loved so much, would then have died completely."

In this short text by St. Augustine many aspects of the behavior of someone who has suffered a great loss are expressed: the disturbance in the way he perceives the world, in that all that was formerly familiar to him becomes a torment. It is as if death had thrown its shadow over everything which was before, even over external things (the house of his father, for example). Here it becomes clear just how much the relationship between two individuals creates a shared world, so that death carries with it the fact that this shared experience of the world is no longer possible. Thus, one aspect of the mourning process must be the creation of /

a new relationship to the world. But still, and this is typical for the first phase following a great loss, St. Augustine is not concerned with creating something new, with searching for something new; on the contrary, he still searches for his friend. Lindemann[2] describes the restlessness of people who have suffered a severe loss: the impulse to do something, to go off in search of something, which is opposed by a lack of goal orientation. Parkes[3] did not see this searching behavior as being goalless, but saw the goal as that of finding the lost partner. St. Augustine appears to have experienced this very consciously.

Thus, to mourning also belongs the task of understanding this restlessness, of comprehending it as an effort to reestablish both the world as it was and to recreate the original relationship structure that was shattered by the death. It must also be understood quite simply as resistance against the change, which life now demands.

St. Augustine describes his condition as sad, confused, "a complete weariness with life side by side with a fear of death," the only relief being weeping. He hated and feared death simultaneously.

In his weariness with life, one sees the extent to which this death event altered his perception of himself and the world: if the friend lives no more, why should he go on living? Yet the fear of death serves to counterbalance these suicidal ideas, as does the thought that, should he himself also die, the friend would be completely dead, because he then could live on in no one's memory.

I feel that hate is also a fundamental part of the process of mourning; in the case of St. Augustine, it is a hatred of death. In my practice as an analyst, I have observed that this hatred is often directed against a godly authority, or against the partner or child who has been lost. Suicidal ideas frequently occur in connection with a great loss. Suicide would be a way of "solving" the many problems that have been caused by the loss. According to a study by Bowlby,[4] the number of individuals who actually commit suicide fol-

13

lowing a death is rather small. On the other hand, the tendency to alleviate the pain through the taking of drugs of all sorts may develop.

To have "a darkness over the heart," to be sad, to be confused, to suffer simultaneously from an aversion to life and a fear of death, to become a living question: all this shows how much not only St. Augustine's perception of the world is shaken, but also his understanding of himself. When St. Augustine says: "... I have experienced his soul and mine as one in two bodies, and for this reason I shuddered in the face of life, because I did not want to live as half a man..." then we can speak of his having suffered a loss of self. It is integral to human life that one's self-perception derives fundamentally from relationships to others, that we often experience as "ourselves" what others have evoked in us and continue to call forth. Our relationship to our innermost self is influenced by the relationships that we have to others, love relationships in particular. In this way a loved one becomes "one half of our soul," belonging in an essential way to our being, determining our feelings toward life and our view of life, without our having the feeling of being manipulated because we have let someone get so close to us that he is a part of ourselves. If we are struck by the loss of someone who is this close, then in fact a part of us also dies.[5] Gabriel Marcel[6] wrote, "The one fundamental problem will be posed by the conflict love-and-death."

Thus the death of one we love is a death problem and an experience of death with which we must come to terms and which we must endure as part of our own passage through life toward our own deaths. It is an extreme life situation which can alter us, but which can set us free to see what is really essential, and it is a situation that can also break us.

Whether we succeed in bringing new perspectives to the way we perceive ourselves and the world, to see consciousness of death also as an aspect of our self-awareness, or whether we collapse, grieve pathologically and never emerge from mourning, is essentially dependent on whether we really understand how to mourn. Grieving should no longer be regarded as a "weakness," but as a psychological process of the greatest importance to the health of a person. For who is spared loss? And if we do not actually have to deal with the death of someone we love, life affords partings enough, and these can bring about loss reactions similar to those which occur when we lose a loved one.

It seems to me important to bear in mind how abruptly the life of a person can change through the death of a life partner, how many difficulties the one left behind is faced with. All this must be coped with in a psychological state of mind that makes problem-solving almost impossible.

Let us once again visualize the problems. Outwardly life changes because a wife becomes a widow; under certain circumstances, she has to struggle with financial problems, with raising the children alone and perhaps with seeking a new partner. Alternatively, if the widow is older, she suddenly has to spend the evening of life alone, perhaps without the necessary practical skills for this, because the husband had always done everything for her. Outwardly life also changes in the sense that a mourner will suddenly be treated in a different way by those around him or her. At worst, the mourner will be tabooed, almost in the same way as death itself; at best he will not be avoided but will be handled "carefully" and unnaturally. People often don't know exactly how to interact with someone who is mourning, and typically they solve this problem by distancing themselves from the mourner. Loneliness is now added to grief and the experience of loss, the feeling of no longer belonging. Parkes[7] in his book dealing with bereavement and life crisis in connection with the loss of a partner, a study of young widows, describes many of these social factors.

The world treats those in mourning in a different way from those who are not mourning. The more grief and death are repressed in a society, the less spontaneously this society will interact with those who mourn and the more quickly

15

this society will demand that one finally put an end to the mourning process.

It is not only that the world approaches the mourner differently; the mourner himself experiences the world in a different way. He has suffered a loss, he is completely preoccupied with a problem that attracts still more problems. He has neither interest nor strength for anything else. He cannot approach others, even when he has an urgent need to do so, precisely because the warmth of others could hinder him from completely losing faith in life. In addition to the fact that no one comes forward to meet him, he cannot approach others who expect that a mourner carry on life in a "normal" way. This happens in our society because we lack a ritualized mourning process, such as still exists, for example, among practicing Jews.[8] In his troubles the mourner distances himself still further and soon experiences the world that he is no longer capable of dealing with as hostile. In this way, a circle of isolation, fear and estrangement from the environment may set in, in which a new attitude toward life can be built up only with difficulty if at all. Paranoid reactions can set in.

The mourner no longer understands the world, and often he does not understand fate any more either. Particularly following the death of those who "die before their time," the meaning of life is questioned: a question to which an answer can hardly be given. In such a situation the stock answers that are offered sound like mockery to the ears of the grieving person and are not much help. It is part of the mourning process to endure this meaninglessness and go on living nevertheless, be it in the hope that meaning will show itself once again, or in remembrance that life was once filled with meaning. Alternatively one can live on courageously in complete doubt as to meaning, existence, God, the human being, or at the very least rendered uncertain by the price that one must pay for the loss of a human bond, and deeply uncertain whether one is ready to pay this price ever again.

But not only these uncertainties as to the meaning of

16

existence plague the mourner; he is truly shaken, changed. His response to life has altered. The way he experiences himself is no longer the same.

A fifty year old man, who lost his wife after a long and difficult illness, described his condition thus:

> "I thought I had prepared myself for the loss. I had had more than enough time to do it. But now that she is dead, I feel that everything is quite different from the way I had imagined it. It is so irretrievable. I sense the magnitude of death; I have learned what is important and what is unimportant. But with what I have learned I can no longer live among others, I have become an eccentric. And then I feel so uncertain. She took so much away from me into the grave, sometimes I ask myself whether enough remains to live."

A forty-five year old woman who had lost her husband in a traffic accident said:

> "It is as if someone had torn him away from me without warning, and I feel as if I am deeply wounded, I am an open wound, I bleed, I am afraid I will bleed to death. But what does it matter, then I will be dead too…"

One may of course assume that this couple had had an especially symbiotic marriage, in which the woman had given up her own personality. But one comes across such statements so frequently, that either everyone carries on a symbiotic partnership, or we are so very dependent on those whom we love in the way we experience ourselves that the death then must be experienced as "a huge hole in me," as a "splintering of my whole personality."

Whatever the reasons for the death of another influencing our perception of ourselves, the grieving one must in time arrive at a unified conception of himself. In all life situations, it seems necessary that we experience ourselves as

17

being at one with ourselves. It is precisely this fragility of self-awareness in the wake of the loss of someone we love which shows how much the relationship to our fellow humans plays a part in our perception of ourselves. This self-perception is also influenced by the core of the personality, thus connected with one's own depths or rooted in a deeper Self. Our self-awareness develops not only out of our first real relationships, important though these might be, but out of all of our relationships. The shattering of self-awareness is difficult to cope with. It seems that precisely mourning and the acceptance of the various emotions that are connected with it, the permitting of oneself to be overwhelmed by senselessness, fear and fury, make it possible for a new self-awareness to come into being. Perhaps grief is the emotion that can create a new order in the life of a stunned individual, a new means of experiencing oneself and the world.

In order that mourning can be accepted, in order that grief can really be experienced, which is psychologically necessary in order to surmount the loss and come to a new understanding of oneself and one's environment, individuals must help one another. Kuhn[9] describes the mourner as feeling like someone who has been expelled from the world: it is not the deceased who is expelled, but the mourner, or, putting it another way, the mourner is expelled along with the deceased. This estrangement has the effect that the mourner then occupies himself excessively with what is past and therefore naturally becomes even more estranged from the real world.

We must find ways to see mourning as something essential, not simply as something pathological, and we must learn again to find ways to mourn with one another. The first step is to overcome our great fear of grief, our tendency to ward it off. In this way we look reality in the eye once again, we experience that we are mortal, that our lives are influenced by many partings, that parting forms part of our being – and that it causes pain. With this also

18

comes the recognition that we are enormously fragile, dependent for our well-being on an endless number of factors which we cannot influence, but at the same time, that we have the capacity to experience and survive grief, that we can experience an extreme situation and be strengthened by it. We must also find new ways to mourn together. We cannot awaken to new life rituals that are no longer valid for us; we will have to find new rituals. Such rituals are, here and there, in the process of being created; apparently we realize that we need them. Schultz[10] writes in his book, *Loneliness,* that, after the death of his wife, many people were around him for many days and that they talked about the deceased among themselves. This seems to me to be a "ritual" that meets the need of the mourner.

I experienced a completely different approach to a new "ritual" at a meeting in which the psyche and death were discussed. In a large group of approximately 120 persons there developed a very intense discussion of death, loss, fear of death, fear of loss, courage in the face of death. A generalized response was evoked without its being embarrassing. Each could identify when he wished, where he wished, where he had been affected in his encounter with death. At the end of the meeting I had the impression that we had mourned together, perhaps precisely because we were actually "strangers" to one another. We had mourned in an especially good way, because to each it was clear that death is something that really plays a role in every life, that each must deal with it in his own way, and that perhaps precisely where we feel the most lonely, we are not so alone. There are many who are grieving with us, if we would only let them approach.

DEATH AND MOURNING
MIRRORED IN A SERIES OF DREAMS

It is known[11] that intensive dreaming occurs in connection with a death event and that the unconscious helps to process the experience. For ten years I have collected the dreams of mourners and found that the unconscious guides the mourning process and in doing so constructs a new identity for the mourning individual. I would like to show the dream series of a young woman as an example of the way in which the unconscious depicts the shock triggered by the death of a loved one and how the essential impulses for coping with the loss came from the dreams. This dream series is very typical. Where necessary, I will occasionally supplement it with examples from the dreams of others in mourning.

The dream series is that of a twenty-five year old woman whom I will call Elena. At the time Elena was a student and very interested in working with the unconscious. She was not, however, undergoing psychotherapeutic treatment. The dream series began before the death of her boyfriend, whom I will call George. George suffered a heart attack and died three weeks later, presumably upon suffering a second attack. Both the first heart attack and the death which followed were unexpected.

On the night before George suffered his first attack Elena dreamt:

"An alpine landscape. I am supposed to go to a specific place. A shy girl about sixteen years old is accompanying me. We are following a chain of high snow-capped mountains, but are ourselves in a green meadow. The

21

sun is warm. Suddenly there is a great rumble, an avalanche falls from one of the peaks and crashes into the valley. The avalanche sweeps rocks and a few trees down with it, then hits some farmers' huts below. We are a few meters away from the edge of the avalanche. There is no danger, but I feel paralyzed. The sun is gone. Suddenly the meadow is strangely gray. We go into one of the huts which remains standing and still seems to be occupied. We must notify the mountain rescue team."

The dream shows an unavoidable natural catastrophe which suddenly breaks into a tranquil alpine scene. The dreamer herself is in no immediate danger, but is nevertheless shaken by this avalanche. This is expressed by the change in the weather: the initial scene is one of warmth, beauty and greenery, which probably indicates a psychological mood of warmth, happiness and growth. The sun vanishes with the fall of the avalanche. It seems to become cold. The pleasure vanishes, bringing a rather joyless atmosphere to the gray scene. A rescue team is required. This dream does not necessarily forecast death, although it concerns the so-called "white death" – an avalanche. As a young girl, Elena was almost caught by an avalanche. Since then she has had a great fear of them. The dream forecasts a natural catastrophe that will bring with it a pronounced change in mood.

Elena associated the alpine landscape with the fact that the Alps make her feel good. She often goes to the Alps when she wishes to find herself; at no other time does she experience her unity as a person so intensely as when she is in the Alps or by the sea. Then she spoke of the last vacation that she had spent in the Alps with George. After she woke up, she stated that the landscape in the dream was completely unknown to her, as was the destination, though in the dream both the path and the destination were familiar to her.

Taking these associations into account, the dream could

announce a "natural catastrophe," that is, a catastrophe for which the individuals involved can scarcely be held responsible: a catastrophe coming from further afield. This catastrophe will affect the dreamer intimately, in the "unity" of her person, in her innermost being. This natural catastrophe might, though must not necessarily, refer to George. It is not clear from the dream what was buried by the avalanche as it is basically a description of an elemental force, which brings with it death but more importantly cold. A rescue team is required, and the dreamer is capable of obtaining this help.

Elena said that, after this dream, she felt as if she was about to die – as if her life were in immediate danger. At first she did not understand the dream. All that she understood was that her life and her feelings toward life were threatened. In addition, she was filled with a feeling of self-pity and pity also for the sixteen year old girl, whom she did not know, but who gave the impression that she had only just begun to live. She told this dream to George, who thought she was overreacting. Something catastrophic might well take place, but neither her life nor the life of the girl who accompanied her were in any way in danger.

The same night before his heart attack, George dreamt:

"The Swiss Army. I am supposed to turn in all my equipment because I am about to undertake a long journey abroad. But I must also hand over my cigarettes, a lighter and a manuscript which I have just begun. I argue that these are my personal property. The officer to whom I must give these things shrugs his shoulders and says, 'That's the way it is here: orders are orders.' I am looking forward to the journey. At last something unpredictable is happening again.

Horses are pulling a heavily laden wagon. Suddenly – I have no idea how – the horses have broken free; the wagon remains standing, then rolls backwards into a tree while the horses gallop away. I am happy that the horses

23

have broken free. They continue to gallop across the
country but cannot harm anyone."

The first dream deals with a preparation for a very long journey. As a Swiss soldier, one must turn in one's military equipment only when planning to take up residence in another country. It is odd, however, that his personal things must also be turned in. Presumably these things were very important to George at the time. In other words, he must leave everything behind and go on a long journey; he looks forward to this, to experiencing something different for once.

In connection with the second dream, George at first recalled a saying from the Chinese book of wisdom, *I Ching,* "Horse and wagon separate, bloody tears flow." In the commentary to this, it states that someone in difficulty shall drop his arms and give up the fight. But George rejected this interpretation immediately on the grounds that his emotions were of a completely different nature: he was happy about the horses, who had their freedom at last. He saw the dream as meaning that he must free himself from his burdens and duties and really make a journey. He had no thoughts about the wagon which rolled into a tree. He understood the dream as a call to make a fundamental change in his life situation.

These dreams can be interpreted in this way, and as long as someone is still alive, he is unwilling to see a forecast of death in them. The long journey with an unknown destination for which one needs no personal property is a possible symbol for the journey into death. But it could just as well be seen as a challenge to discover something entirely new in oneself. In George's dreams can be seen what I already had seen from time to time in the dreams of individuals whose deaths were imminent: the dreams speak of something new, something longed for or sometimes anxiously awaited – without one's being able to make out whether this 'something new' signifies death or simply something new in this world.

Elena and George attempted to find the connection between their dreams. George felt his dream showed very clearly that he had to break out again and go on a long journey, perhaps even without Elena; yes, it actually seemed that it would be better to do this without Elena. Naturally this would be a catastrophe for her. Elena remarked dryly: a catastrophe, to be sure, but not a natural catastrophe. She was afraid that something would happen to him, that he could be ill. George replied thoughtfully that he did, in fact, feel peculiar that day, strange somehow, but that he just needed to unwind.

The next dream Elena remembered occurred three days after George's heart attack. George is still alive.

"I am standing on a threshold. A calf must be killed on this threshold, and no blood may spill onto the floor in the process; all the blood must be caught. I try with the greatest care to catch all the blood in a basin. It is a tremendous quantity of blood. It flows and flows. I become increasingly sickened. I feel ill. I awaken."

After this dream, Elena, already very worried about George, though the doctors assured her that he was in no immediate danger, felt "miserable as never before in my entire life." She felt powerless, overwhelmed, but said that the dream also had a "strangely sacred" quality. The seriousness, the care with which she had caught the blood in the basin, had reminded her of a sacred act. But this was only *one* feeling. The feeling of wretchedness was far more distinct, far more agonizing, and it was probably that which woke her up.

The threshold suggests a transition: standing at the threshold, standing on the threshold. At this point of transition the killing of the calf must take place, the calf must be sacrificed. This image reminds one of the animal sacrifice which we know from the Old Testament.

According to the old belief, the blood is the resting place of the soul. It must not be lost because it belongs to God. However, the form in which the soul existed must be killed, must be sacrificed, a transformation must take place. The dreamer associated the calf with joy of living, vitality, freedom from restraint, naive pleasure in existence. The calf suggests youth. (Luther once said, "You still have a lot of calf flesh!") Elena must sacrifice this youthful, light-hearted vitality and joy in living without losing its essence, the blood. A dreadful sacrifice is required of the dreamer; no wonder she feels ill. The sacrifice takes the last of her strength. The streaming blood shows the fullness of her warm emotionality which is shed and must be saved. The collecting of the blood in a basin struck Elena as being "strangely sacred." This preserving of the essence at the command of someone who is not present – Elena simply *knows* that this has to happen – has not only the quality of a task almost impossible to accomplish but also the quality of something sacred, something meaningful, even if the dreamer cannot read any immediate meaning into it.

The dream indicates that a threshold must be crossed by Elena, that a step toward maturity is required of her. The step is a difficult one because it involves a tremendous sacrifice of youthfulness, vitality, sexuality and warmth. None of this may actually be lost, it is part of her innermost being, but it must be lived in another form.

Elena understood the dream as a reaction to her life situation, which had changed dramatically. The man she loved was in hospital and his life was in danger. She understood that she must be more adult and that the relationship must change. She thought it nevertheless strange, even at that stage, that she should find this as difficult as the dream seemed to show. Then she added: "Actually, from this dream, one could think that I am the one who is about to die." The dream certainly indicates that a transformation will be demanded of her. But the dream-ego does not die, it participates in death via the calf which must be slaughtered and whose blood must be collected. The dream also contains an allusion to the future, for if death alone were signified, then the blood could simply be allowed to spill.

Three days before his death George dreamt:

"I see a forest over which a storm must have broken. The pines are lying this way and that. Lumberjacks are there. They are loading the trees and carrying them away. I wonder why the forest, which seems so strong, could not withstand the storm. I watch sadly."

Once again in this dream we encounter a natural force which this time has broken over a forest. And the forest, which appeared so solid, just as George appeared so solid, was destroyed. A tree that falls can be, among other things, an image for someone who dies; in any event, it is an image of crushed vitality. George himself asked whether this dream could herald his approaching death. Almost immediately, however, he thought that it could also mean that something must be cleared away, that the after-effects of his illness must be cleared away, so that he could begin life anew.

Both interpretations are possible; nevertheless, George focused first on the fact that the dream could be heralding death. George shows by his interpretation that he is oriented toward death, but also toward the possibility of recovery.

In the dream he looks on sadly. Kübler-Ross[12] established that certain phases through which the mourner passes are also experienced by the dying before death. This process of mourning was in George's case not visible as a complete process. He had too little time left. Apparent in his case was the phase of denial, which surfaced in the dream of the "journey," and also in his reaction to Elena's dream of a natural catastrophe. Here in this last dream sadness played an important role. When he told the dream to Elena, he said that the dream had filled him with an immeasurable sadness, and then he spoke of parting. This upset him. He

27

listed all the things he would still like to do, named those with whom he was furious, with whom he had not been fair, but also said how fine life had been. He recounted episodes which had made life worth living. Even if coming to terms with death had hardly been possible for George, in the sense that it is perhaps possible for those who approach death more slowly, the first phases of mourning seemed in evidence.

The night before George's death Elena dreamt:

"I see a monitor screen. The upper half is bright, the lower half is darker. Three beams of light run across this screen, from right to left. After one beam of light crosses a third of the screen, it drops suddenly, as though extinguished. Then I realize that it is continuing its path down below in the darker half. I think of George and am frightened. The second beam begins to flicker, but settles again. Someone says that is Mrs. X.'s beam. (This woman had had a heart attack some time before, but had recovered.) The third beam of light also begins to flicker and disappears off the end of the screen. Instinctively, I know that this light beam is that of Mrs. A, a woman to whom I am very close. (This woman died young four years later.) I wake up and am deeply disturbed."

Naturally Elena thought immediately of George, whose heart function had been monitored on a screen for some time. It was clear to her that the dream had not communicated the real sign of heart failure, but for her the plunge of the beam of light meant the death of this man who had come to represent something like a light for her. The dream did not speak of a plunge into nothingness, but rather of a fall into another sphere, in which the light beam continued on its way, though scarcely visible any more. One beam of light is identified with Frau X and therefore confirms that the dream deals with the issue of death.

Elena said that she knew then that George would die.

28

She also thought the dream wanted to say that death is not simply death, but that the light continues, only in such a way that we can scarcely perceive it.

This dream was a great comfort to Elena for a long time. Previously she was loath to make any statement regarding life after death and dismissed speculation on this theme as a cheap attempt to conquer fear. Now suddenly as a result of this dream she was convinced that someone whom one has loved cannot die, that he lives on in some form not recognized, or scarcely recognized, by our limited consciousness.

If we look at the three dreams Elena had before George's death as related, then it becomes apparent that the dreams are preparing the way for *the* great separation, presenting it as a catastrophe and showing what a tremendous change will be demanded of Elena. Elena's reaction to the first two dreams, the feeling that she herself was threatened by death, seems clearly to indicate just to what extent we do "die with" the loved one. The dreams afford little comfort other than to indicate that Elena will not die herself, that she is just strong enough to bear the onslaught of something frightful. A small comfort lay perhaps in the fact that, though she experienced the collecting of the blood as terrible, it was also experienced as something "strangely sacred." She could find meaning in that. The last dream indicated that the hour of death had arrived. It was comforting for Elena in as far as it gave her the chance to develop a philosophy of life in which the dead, even if in a way not easily recognized, continue to be with us. This dream, which of course simultaneously stressed the inevitability of fate, already "anticipated" the task of mourning. Because the dreamer had already had an image of life after death, the way was prepared for the searching behavior that always follows a loss.[13]

Schelling[14] wrote a paper after the death of his wife, Caroline (1809), "The Connection between Nature and the Spirit World," (1810-11). The pain he experienced over the death of his wife led him to reflect upon death: "Nothing can engage me nor console me henceforth but dealings with the subjects of a higher world, by which I dispel the pain of the painful separation." In his ponderings he came to the conclusion that " 'in our innermost being' we remain united with the deceased ..."

Similarly, Gabriel Marcel[15] went even further when he said, "The being that I love is still there, even though dead."

It is easy to imagine that an individual whom we have loved still lives on with us as long as he survives in our memory. It cannot be overlooked, however, that the absence of the physical presence changes this relationship totally. The mourner may attempt to maintain contact with the deceased by means of a religious philosophy or perhaps in sessions with a spiritualist. But it is the loss of the physical presence which reminds one painfully of the death of the loved one and makes clear the fundamental difference from the time of his physical existence.

In the night following George's death, Elena dreamt:

"I embrace George, I feel very close to him and am overcome by feelings of tenderness. Suddenly I feel him become colder and colder. He dies in my arms. I am filled with despair. I know that nothing can bring him back again, that I can no longer embrace him, no longer feel him."

In this dream Elena again experiences the death event with intensity. At first the physical togetherness is described as wonderful, but then the dream shows that it is precisely this kind of togetherness which is no longer possible. It also shows that it is through this that Elena realizes that George has died. It may be that this dream offsets the fantasies that Elena had had in connection with the dream about the fall of the beam of light, fantasies along the lines that the dead continue to live in a certain way. This last dream now states clearly: that way is not a physical one. The dream

30

might also compensate for Elena's waking state shortly after George's death. Like everyone else, she did not want to acknowledge it. Immediately after George's death she was numb, devoid of feeling. She did what needed to be done like an automaton and repeatedly told herself that she must be dreaming, that this must definitely be a terrible dream. But she knew full well that it was no dream, but rather a terrible reality, from which she must awake one day.

This phase of denial, the paralysis, the lack of feeling, is designated in a very general way as the first phase of the mourning which follows a great loss.[16] It is also the first phase of the mourning process which someone undergoes upon learning that he, in all probability, suffers from an incurable disease.[17]

The dream could have the function of preparing the dreamer to accept the loss. Obviously, at this point Elena cannot yet accept it but it seems to me that the dream indicates that the death and the fundamental change in this relationship, i.e., the physical absence, must be accepted. Most authors who deal with death and mourning agree that, when the death is really accepted, perhaps even a meaning found in it, the process of mourning is completed.[18]

Two days after George's death Elena dreamt:

"I receive a big parcel of letters. They are the letters that I have written to George. I know that it is not nearly all of them, it is only the ones which still bother me somewhat. There is also a letter from George among them. He writes, 'You cannot imagine how wonderful it was as I followed that banner.' He had drawn the banner: it was a blue flag with a crown, and fire under the crown. On the one hand I was happy about the letter, but on the other hand I was sad and above all furious because he had left me on account of this banner."

Letters had played a very important role in the relationship between Elena and George. They loved to write to one

31

another of little everyday events, and Elena wrote to George often, sometimes several times a day, especially during his time in the hospital.

What Elena had given to George – the letters, their communications, the expression of their love and their relationship – was returned to her. These letters still concern her, suggesting that this love could not simply die with the partner. She must note once more what was essential for them both and what was essential for her personally, for they are the letters that *she* wrote.

In this part of the dream there is also the suggestion that the return of the letters is a symbol for the breaking-off of a relationship through death. Elena does not receive all the letters, but only those which bother her, which stresses that she should take note once again of what was important for her in this relationship and should realize that all the love that was expressed in these letters is not simply lost. This would correspond to the blood in the dream of the calf, the blood that must not be left to flow away and the value which is not lost.

George tells her that he followed a banner. He seems to have followed something that was very important to him. The crusader in him is revealed: following a banner, putting himself at the service of an idea, and unconditionally (as is expressed by the banner). But which idea is expressed?

The blue background of the flag could represent a spiritual passion. It could be said that this spiritual passion was the leading factor in his life, symbolizing perhaps the culmination of that life. The individualistic design of the banner which he followed seems to point to his individual destiny, which he also followed. For the dreamer this part of the dream was a sign that death really was George's destiny, that it was *his* death, and that it had a meaning. For Elena it was a message from the other side, a message which at first made her very happy. One can, however, with equal justification say that this dream segment represents her own intuitive feelings about the background to his

32

death and that her psyche is searching for a meaning in it. Elena would like to understand, because she does not understand this death.

Also essential for Elena was the fact that the emotions evoked in this dream – joy, grief and fury – be preserved after waking. Joy that the relationship did not simply come to an end, because Elena had been afraid of this after the dream of the previous night. Grief, because George had nevertheless died. Fury at being abandoned while he followed his own destiny, his banner, even joyfully. This dream initiated a phase in which the dreamer experienced all of these emotions with intensity, though especially fury at the fact that he had left her. It was also her philosophy that one must of course follow one's highly individual destiny; she too could see the sense in that. She recognized that she could not now pass judgment on this pursuit of one's own destiny, a trait which she had loved so much in George while he lived. Nevertheless, she was grief-stricken and furious. The dream was instrumental in helping her to leave the first phase of mourning after George's death, the phase of absolute numbness that accompanied the denial that he had died. It brought her into the second phase of mourning, in which the emotions of grief and anger could find expression.

During this time Elena was often among friends who had known them both and whom she had called upon to help her. In their many conversations they tried to discuss the deceased and encourage Elena not to idealize George but also to recognize those aspects of him that could make her furious. There was, for instance, his selfishness in saying he must follow his own destiny, while failing to consider the relationship with Elena. In these discussions it became clear that it is not at all easy to "speak ill" of the dead. The maxim, "Don't speak ill of the dead" is firmly rooted in us. Though we are well aware of how unsound this maxim is and how far it hinders our coming to terms with the deceased we still tend to idealize the dead. The circle of friends was addicted to talking about George (about his heroic deeds, his idiosyncrasies, etc.) as if in this way they would not lose him completely. This discussion of the deceased following the death seems to have several functions. On the one hand, the emotions that are bound up with the deceased are aroused and can, and must be, expressed. The problems that still exist with respect to the deceased can then be cleared up. Feelings of anger at being abandoned can also be brought to expression here. These discussions seem to have the function of "finding" the deceased. For if the deceased is "sought" by the mourner, and this is only natural since we, as humans, respond to loss with searching, then this searching phase signifies that we have not yet come to terms with the loss.

After Elena had accepted the fact that George was dead at least outwardly and had awakened from her numbed state, "attacks" of anger at fate, aggression towards a life that can only let its creations die, alternated with phases of quiet grief. She experienced herself for the most part as out of control. And she was, but that is a good pre-condition for coming to terms with a loss experience. What was missing in Elena's case, in comparison with most mourning processes, were feelings of guilt. This might be accounted for by the fact that in the relationship between Elena and George it would be discussed very openly if one or the other of the partners felt 'victimized.' In addition it was clear to both that no relationship can be lived without indebtedness to one another. Self-reproach did not grow out of all proportion, for Elena was of the opinion that she had done everything she could have done in this situation.

Elena came across to others as composed. There was, however, this entry in her diary: "I am very glad for the support of my friends. I have the feeling that I need people around me to hold my body together, otherwise I could fall apart." Elena thus sensed acutely the threat to the unity of her person; she needed the warmth of human contact to endure this threat.

34

A week after George's funeral, which Elena had experienced as being of no particular value to either the dead or the living, she dreamt:

"I am waiting for George. He comes and sits down on a bench under a tree. He hands me a sheet of paper on which there is brown writing, but in mirror image. It is the draft for a scientific paper. I hope that I can read it. Apart from this George gives me a rubber band. I look at him somewhat puzzled and ask: 'What am I supposed to do with this bequest?' I am angry at my own lack of tact in reminding him of his death. You see, throughout the dream I am aware that we have buried him. But I also see that he is very much alive."

Presumably this dream is concerned with the bequest of the dead: a scientific paper – one that cannot be simply accepted but must be mirrored, reflected, until it is readable and therefore understandable.

Elena had no idea what the significance of the draft paper was. The brown color of the writing is interesting. Brown as the color of the earth, the mother, in the context of death naturally also the color of the earth that covered the coffin. Does this sheet indicate that it is simply one of George's ideas which was still lying around and upon which, as one could imagine, he might like someone who was familiar with his interests to complete work? Or was it really a formula that had some connection with his death? For Elena, the dream's message was clear: George would continue to play from the other side of the grave the extraordinarily stimulating role that he had played in her life. But she was not able to simply accept this impulse; she would have to reflect it and translate it into human terms. She also concluded from this that the world after death could be a mirror image of our world. The rubber band she saw as the chance of a further connection between the two, but a flexible, rather than a fixed one.

During this period Elena tended to perceive the dream image of George as an objective and real figure, attempting to deliver messages to her from the realm of the dead. These nightly meetings with George comforted her a great deal but always plunged her back into mourning. It is clear from the dreams, however, that her dream-ego also strives for detachment. She reminds George again and again that he is dead; she reminds *herself* in this way of the fact that it really is an altered relationship.

Looking at this dream from the outside, one is inclined to perceive the figure of George as representative of what has grown within her as a result of the relationship to George. If this is the case, the dream is saying that – although he is certainly dead – that which has grown within her continues to live, to motivate her and to convey to her the sense of a bond even though, in more concrete terms, contact has been severed. The dream seems to transmit this double meaning very clearly: on the one hand, the knowledge that the relationship has been broken off, and on the other, the perception that what was brought into being by the relationship continues to make itself felt and wants to be realized. From this point of view it would be useful if Elena would work out some concept of George's, thereby transforming the role of the initiator, which until now she had projected onto him, into her own potential to initiate.

In this dream, it seems to me that the search for George continues. It can be seen not only as a resistance to accepting the loss, but also as an attempt to find in oneself that which had developed in the course of the relationship with the deceased. Discovering what was unique in the relationship is an essential aspect of one's own self-perception, which must be built up again. It is simply not true that, when someone dies, the time spent with them is merely erased. On the contrary, the time spent with someone, the aspects of life lived or not lived together, will become evident upon the death of this person.

That Elena, at this point in time, regarded the dream figure of George as a real visitation from the Hereafter shows that for her the search still took place on a very real level. If the aim was not entirely to reestablish the old relationship, it was nevertheless to make the least possible change in the face of death. This behavior is typical. Bowlby and Parkes mention different mourning processes in which, during the phase of searching, the deceased partner is either perceived as altogether real, even if not visibly present, or as someone who now existed in the Hereafter but who could nevertheless communicate with one at any time. This experience cannot really be contradicted, but that does not mean that general statements about life after death can be based on it. As long as a person continues to have an intense relationship with the deceased, who remains so alive in the psyche that even dialogue is possible, then the mourner will never be content with the idea that it is only a memory. The fantasy can be of tremendous value, but of course cannot be compared with the dialogue as it existed before the partner's death. The presence of the deceased is of a radically different kind, even though it is still experienced as a presence. It is precisely this radical alteration which must be accepted, step by step, in the mourning process. The danger lies in the fact that the one who is grieving tries to rescue whatever can be rescued of what was once familiar. This might be very comforting in the short term, but it can prolong the process of mourning.

Elena dreamt three weeks after George's funeral:

"George writes me a letter. He asks me to visit him and names a train station on the border as the meeting place. I meet him. We are in a train together with others. At a certain place we must all climb out, only George may and must travel on. I attempt by means of the highest authority to arrange that I might also go on, that I might travel with George – but to no avail: the authority wants nothing to do with me.

37

Tenderly, we say good-bye – I feel numb.
Now I have to find a train to travel back. I search end-
lessly, running from station to station. All night long I
feel like l have been searching for the right train. Then at
some point, I find myself in a train that is going back.
There are a lot of people in this train: I am afraid of these
people – also, there is no room for me. I end up between
two train carriages and wake up completely exhausted..."

Elena must now separate even more radically from
George, but this separation takes place via a meeting. In this
contact and the separation required in spite of it we see the
entire paradox of this phase of mourning: we must occupy
ourselves with the deceased. It is essential to let the positive
feelings for them be felt again, to keep on experiencing the
bond which again and again brings temporary respite from
the difficult searching process. When such reunions take
place in dreams,it can have a very beneficial effect on the
state of mind of the mourner.[19] But at the same time we
must create a distance between ourselves and the dead.
There must be a genuine acceptance of the leave-taking.
Presumably, we can do this only when we begin to see the
deceased as a figure within us.

The separation announces itself in the meeting place
specified by the dream: a train station on the border. Once
again, a border must be crossed. At this border crossing
George must go further than anyone else. The dreamer
would like to share the journey into death, the journey into
the Hereafter, with the man she loves. Elena feels at this
time a very strong pull toward "the other side" – not that she
actively would have wanted to end her life, but rather that
she was incredibly indifferent to danger. As Bowlby has
also observed, this too seems to be a typical characteristic of
mourners, at least in the early phases of mourning.[20] What
value has life for her now that the loved one has died? It
seems to me also to indicate the shock to one's identity:
what will *my* life be worth after this loss?

But in the dream Elena was sent back. It was difficult enough for her to find the right train, and at first, she did not want to go back at all; she wanted to prevail upon the "highest authority" to let her go with George. This "highest authority" reminded Elena of a book by Kasack,[21] *The City Beyond the River,* that she had once read. Similarly, this book was about a journey across a river into the land of the dead. In this story, too, one needed permission from a mysterious "high commissioner" to be able to live in that land on the other side. Elena remembered that the book described how someone who was still living was bidden to come to this city beyond the river in order to manage the archives in which everything relating to the spiritual existence of humankind was stored. She remembered also that this archivist was then able to pursue once again a love relationship with a woman who had died. He eventually came back again and travelled throughout the land in a train, speaking to those who were willing to listen to him. She knows that, in this book, it states that the more people learn about death and the deceased, the more they develop a trust in life.

Elena appears to identify with this archivist to some extent. Would she simply like to die, or would she, like the archivist, wish to accompany her beloved for a time in death and then return to tell people what she had learnt? It appears to me that, in this wish, a wish for something grandiose seems to be hidden, finding expression in the idea that a highest authority, with whom she is not even granted a hearing, must be consulted. The need for a tremendous experience is easy to understand in the light of her feeling that her person has been shattered. A great experience could, with a single stroke, lead to a new self-awareness. But Elena must turn back at the border.

The return trip is difficult. In the dream Elena feels unsure of the other people around her. That is the way she feels in reality, too. The time in which friends could help her in her mourning is past. Elena does not venture in this phase to ask for further support; she realizes that she must, in the end, come to terms with things herself. But she doesn't come to terms with them. She is occupied with death, with questions that deal with life after death. Messages in dreams about George are interpreted as information that he is sending to her from that world on the other side. Because of this preoccupation, she develops a strong yearning for the Hereafter and, to a great extent, neglects contact with the living.

But the dream now refers her back to the living. She still finds no place among them: she finds herself "between the carriages of the train," again in a transition, but the train is nevertheless returning. This longing for the other side, the wish to die too, must be sacrificed. She must let George go, she must let him go his way, a way which will lead ever further away from her own path. Her path leads in exactly the opposite direction, but she must go her own way. She will meet George, find joy in this, accept the parting, mourn. Only then can she make the separation.

This seems to be a sequence which reveals itself repeatedly in the mourning process: the memory of the deceased will again come to life, and pleasures will be reexperienced, along with anger, fear and grief. But precisely because of this it will be possible to distance oneself a bit further from the deceased as a 'real' person. At the same time, that which had bound the mourner to the deceased is more consciously integrated into the mourner's psyche. It becomes a personal experience which can no longer be taken away, not even by death.

After this dream Elena didn't feel well at all. Its message was clear but she experienced in reality what she had experienced in the dream: she didn't exactly know how she should return to the real world. There was nothing that would have bound her or even interested her. The world of the living seemed trivial to her. Listlessly, she occupied herself once again with her studies. After a few weeks, however, she surprised her friends with the news that she had signed up for the final examinations.

Approximately one year later she mentioned how important this dream had been for her – how important it had also been for her to experience this "border situation." It had saved her life. At the time that she had the dream she had simply felt rejected, but she noticed after a while how clearly life stretched before her, how she could suddenly discriminate the unimportant from the important.

This dream was certainly of decisive importance, turning Elena back to face her own world. It shows that when one's world is shattered by the death of a loved one, in Elena's case to the extent that she was ready to give up her own life, then the unconscious works to recreate an awareness of world and self independent of the one that has been lost. At the same time her reaction to the dream indicates the way life suddenly receives a different emphasis through the experience of its extreme limits, and that, through this, what is incidental and cumbersome can be cast off.

There followed now a period in which Elena prepared herself for the examinations with great care. Otherwise she still grappled with the loss of George whenever feelings related to the loss overcame her, as a result of a dream or because something in real life reminded her of him. She allowed herself to experience these moments of grief and sadness. The dreams in this phase brought her many memories of George; problems that she had had with him would suddenly surface again in a dream, as though he were still alive. An example of a dream from this phase:

"I am sitting with George in the car. He is driving like a madman; at the same time, he is developing an idea for better use of the roads. He accompanies this by gesticulating argumentatively with his hands and feet. I become furious, snapping at him that he should concentrate – pay more attention to the traffic – otherwise he can hatch a scheme for the better handling of accident victims. George laughs and drives even faster. I begin to stroke

41

him, whereupon he slows down. I am furious about his
obstinacy, yet proud that I can handle him."

This dream takes up a problem that Elena and George had had: George liked to drive very fast, and it was his custom when driving fast to develop at the same time some concept or other, clear up philosophical issues, etc. Elena believed this to be doing too much at once. She was afraid. Her behavior in the dream corresponds to her real behavior: at first she scolded angrily, which had never worked. Then she tried to soothe George with tenderness. Elena always found this behavior of George's selfish, even suicidal. Her own behavior she also found poor, because she had manipulated him out of her own powerlessness.

Dreams of this sort always caused Elena to think over the relationship she had with George and the way she behaved towards him. In time she began to see George more realistically, with his shortcomings as well as his merits.

Naturally one asks whether such dreams are not also to be understood at the subjective level:[22] George would then not be interpreted as the real George – as he was – but rather as an aspect of the personality of Elena. It is presumably appropriate to see the dreams at the subjective as well as at the objective level, in each case within the context of a reappraisal of the relationship. It seems important not to interpret the dreams of mourners too quickly on the subjective level, which regards the partner as an aspect of the dreamer. This could prevent a full awareness of the relationship. It seems important for the emerging self-awareness that the dreamer sees how he or she behaved within the relationship. After all, the behavior patterns of the mourner also played a part in forming the relationship. The absence of the partner allows these behavior modes to be seen with a clarity hardly possible otherwise.

Approximately three months after George's death Elena dreamt:

"George is lying in a wooden coffin which is open. I can see him lying there as if he is sleeping. I must place some sort of herb on him as a medicine. Doctors are also there; they are running busily here and there with case histories under their arms, although there is nothing at all to be done. In answer to my question about what they are waiting for, they reply that George could wake up at any time.

Greatly cheered, I look spellbound at the coffin. George really does begin to move slowly, turning from his side onto his back. He rubs his eyes, sees me, greets me and says, 'You know, that wasn't at all funny.' By that he obviously means the time spent in the coffin. He stands up, reassures the doctors and says that he wants first of all to take a walk with me in the woods.

We leave. I hear a piece of music that featured largely in the time we shared together. I walk by his side and wonder whether this is now the ghost of George and why spirits are so very physical. George says, 'Now I can stay here with you.' I find that very nice but notice that our relationship is greatly changed: I experience him as if he were a part of me. On the walk we meet friends of mine; we continue together, picking up more and more people along the way."

If the theme in the dream of the border train station was a separation and genuine acceptance of the fact that the deceased has a different path than the one who stays behind, then this dream deals with coming together again, albeit in a new way: "Our relationship is greatly changed: I experience him as if he were a part of me." That George lies in a coffin can also be a sign that Elena has really accepted George's death. The open wooden coffin could indicate that she can look upon the face of the dead, that she can really confront this death.

The wooden coffin is also called "the tree of the dead" in Switzerland. Its connection to a hollowed-out tree trunk is thus made plain: the coffin that is fashioned from the wood of a tree, the maternal hollow shelter that receives the dead – and can indicate a transformation.

In our dream this transformation takes place. At first one sees hope for this transformation. What could move the dream-ego to lay on herbs if this hope did not exist? The doctors with the case histories also hope for a transformation, they even speak of it. It is certainly healing for the dreamer when this man gets up. By this I mean that these doctors are concerned at least as much with the dream-ego as with George.

In the dream a resurrection takes place. Again one can interpret this resurrection in two ways. Elena takes it to mean that George, now dead, has behind him the first phase of transformation, and for this reason, he can once again be near her. Such an explanation cannot be proven, nor can it be refuted. But everyone who has lost someone probably accepts the appearance of the dead in dreams as real.

The resurrection can also be seen as an indication that Elena is entering a new phase in her mourning for George. "... that wasn't at all funny" might also be true for Elena: the time George was really in the coffin, thus really dead, was certainly very difficult for her. If the train dream expressed, among other things, that she still simply wanted to *have* George but that she must let him go, then this dream shows that she now may experience George near to her again. Perhaps for the very reason that she no longer clung to him so tightly she has become free for another type of relationship. This is also expressed in the dream by the music that symbolizes their feeling of belonging together. "Now I can stay here with you" could mean that it is now possible for Elena to retain on an emotional level that which George had meant to her, to live it herself, to be in contact with it.

In this way a new orientation with respect to life may follow, not in the sense that she forgets the relationship and the sadness caused by it, but rather in the sense that this relationship has now become a part of her. The new orientation is also seen in that friends appear in the dream. The way to others is open again, in contrast to the train dream in which she was afraid of others.

Dreams in which the dead rise from the coffin seem to be common. I have observed them, with variations, in twelve individuals who had lost someone who was very close to them. The Christian idea of resurrection may of course play a part here, but this does not lessen the personal significance of these dreams. It would only mean that these thoughts of resurrection are a fundamental part of our psyche.

The dream of a fifty-one year old woman was another on this theme:

"I am trying to park at Enge Train Station. Getting out of the car, I see approximately twenty meters in front of me an open coffin. I know that Helmut is lying in it. I know that he has already been dead for fifty days and must be quite decomposed, but I have to take a look anyway. I am afraid. I come closer. The coffin is no longer there, but Helmut is lying there in the open in his long dark-green dressing gown. I can't see his face, or perhaps I don't dare look, but I want to touch the body. Then he moves and turns over in that unmistakable way he had. We look at each other without saying a word, then I go away filled with a mixture of consternation and satisfaction."

As in Elena's dream the deceased, who is at first "turned away," turns again toward his wife. The fact that they look at one another seems important. Presumably they both need to take in the new situation.

Parkes[23] mentions a similar dream:

"He was in the coffin with the lid off, when all of a sudden he came to life and got out. I was so overjoyed to

45

think that he was here that, when I woke up, I wondered where he could be. It was so clear that I had to laugh and cry at the same time. I looked at him and he opened his mouth. I said, 'He's alive! He's alive!' I thought, 'Thank God, I'll have him to talk to again.' "

Parkes maintains that this is a typical dream in dealing with loss to be understood purely in terms of wish-fulfillment – though that seems to me too limited an interpretation. Even if wish-fulfillment is mirrored in it, it seems important nevertheless to look at this dream on the subjective level also. It is important to see that, at the same time, it ends a phase of mourning by announcing that the deceased can now once again be "part of the mourner's life" though in a different way.

The difference between Elena's dream and that of the London widow lies in the fact that it seems clear to Elena, even in the dream, that another sort of relationship now exists between her and the deceased partner. Helmut's wife also walks away, "consterned and satisfied," from the "resurrected" Helmut. But there is certainly no question of reestablishing the relationship in its old form.

It seems to me that when this type of dream occurs it marks a turning point in the experience with the death. The dreamer feels that life can continue once again; a new understanding of himself and the world has developed. It becomes clear that a great deal that appeared to be lost when the loved one died lives on, at least partly, in the one left behind and can also be realized by him. The mourner becomes aware that a great deal which was formerly "outside," that is, experienced in the relationship, has not simply vanished, but now can and must be internalized.

This can of course only be grasped if the process of mourning "succeeds."[24] If the mourning succeeds, then the death of a loved one can contribute in an essential way to self-realization, to individuation. The death forces one to determine, so to speak, what in a relationship is really one's own.

A dream of Elena's half a year after the death of George:

"I am at a spa. I am walking badly because I have apparently fractured and wounded my right leg, and I am here to heal it. I think: I must have been in an avalanche, and it strikes me as remarkable that I didn't die in it.

The dream image changes: still at the spa, in the warm water. George is there and I am arguing with him about 'meaning.' My argument is: life can't possibly have a meaning if the people whom one loves die, while the people whom one doesn't love continue to live. George attempts to convince me that, precisely because of death, life has a meaning. I am annoyed and tell him that is just talk. When he died, it seemed to me that life was not worth living, but had become a damned burden for me to carry. I dive away.

Suddenly I know that there is something in the life of every human being that transcends the here and now. It can't be formulated, but suddenly, I am filled with the strong feeling that to focus oneself upon this fact gives a meaning to life.

I climb out of the bath. An older woman is there and says: 'Suddenly, you have completely different eyes.' 'Yes,' I say, 'something in me just died.' I say this with a beaming face. She looks at me somewhat perplexed."

In the meantime, Elena had attempted to live as normally as possible. She met with her friends and concluded her studies. To those who knew her better, she came across as rather joyless, strained, depressive and enormously brave. Conversations which she initiated often circled around the meaning of life.

The dream says at the beginning that the dreamer must be healed further: in a medicinal bath. Medicinal baths are reminiscent of the state within the womb, of that cozy existence in warm water. For the very reason that this regression is allowed, the medicinal bath has a healing effect.

The disintegration, the wounding that Elena suffered through the death of George, was represented by the fractured bones and wounds of the right leg. It is with our legs that we stand on the ground. They give us both a firm foothold and the option of movement. Thus Elena no longer had either a firm foothold or mobility. "Right" most often means the side that is turned toward the world, toward consciousness. This side was supposedly affected most. When we look at Elena's dreams, it becomes clear that her relationship with her inner self was not broken off at all, but had in fact been strengthened by the loss; it was contact to the outside world which had been broken. It is interesting that this dream again takes up the motif of the avalanche, which featured in the first dream; a circle has probably been completed.

In the second dream picture it is clear at another level what it is that must be healed: not simply the leg, but rather her despair over the question of meaning.

What George says is true in an abstract way: "In the face of death" she can be happy that she is alive, but she cannot be happy that she is alive if someone to whom she is closely bound is taken away from her by death. The thought of death, and of dying with the loved one, is here far stronger than the joy at continuing to exist.

This ambivalence also seems to me to be typical of someone who has experienced the loss of a loved one, but only in the phase in which the loss can be accepted. Life is no longer simply a burden. Life can once again be enormously colorful and worth living when one takes a firm stand against death. At the same time the mourner knows that, in a sense, she has also died with the loved one, that she must also be reborn, born again into life.

The change of location in this dream appears to be very important: in the first part of the dream, the dreamer is simply at a spa; in the second part, clearly in warm water. She even dives beneath the surface, and in so doing, experiences meaning, in the feeling that every life extends far beyond existence in the here and now. Perhaps this is what is meant by an inclusion of the death experience in her own life. She then emerges, apparently born anew. This submersion and re-emergence express her transformation, death and rebirth.

As a result her eyes are changed. In the eyes, emotional changes are easily seen. This is confirmed by the dreamer when she says that something in her has just died. She has dived beneath the surface and in doing so has lost the tormenting feeling of senselessness. This feeling has "died." As a result Elena has "died into life," because to experience the new meaning emotionally means to have regained faith in life, a life which has death in store, as she has so painfully experienced. And now, changed, she can climb out of the medicinal bath. One stage in the healing process is completed. She will certainly have to be "healed" again from time to time, but the essential step toward healing is nevertheless taken at the moment when the dreamer is flooded with this sense of meaning.

This dream brought Elena a new joy in life. She felt she had accomplished something great, and she certainly had. She had faced up to a process of mourning, and as a result, she can live on; she can enjoy life again. More importantly, the awareness of death has become a dimension of her own self-consciousness.

To me, this dream series is remarkable because the process of mourning was guided by the dreams and because, from these dreams, we are shown how to mourn. These dreams lead so "beautifully" through the mourning process and in the end, cause an essential dimension to be included in Elena's life as a result of the death of a loved one and the processing of the loss experience. It should not, however, be overlooked that Elena had at first experienced the death as a catastrophe bringing her to the brink of death herself. Only endurance of the catastrophe, the bearing of the shock, led to the transformation.

Catastrophe and transformation are part of the death of someone we love. If we see only the catastrophic aspect of death, then we must repress it, because it is too horrifying. In doing so we also repress mourning, because it causes us too much pain, and this repression leads to various psychological problems (which will be discussed later). If we see only the catastrophic aspect, we are likely either to flee into "activity as a means of resisting death,"[25] or the feeling is transferred so that we can no longer let go of anything. If we see only the transformative aspect of death, we forget what immense pain and uncertainty it can unleash. We become too romantic, even to the point of craving death, and we begin to let go of everything too quickly.

What was said here about death of course does not refer only to the ultimate death of an individual. We experience death in many aspects: in loss of any sort, disappointment, failure, parting, withdrawal, climax, or striving for permanence. All these things and many more have something to do with death. More than anything, the breaking-off of a relationship can release similar desperation and can shake the way we experience ourselves in a way very similar to the real death of a partner. The conflict between love and death is always present, though in the case of a real death, it is experienced most intensely. An essential aspect of life is the necessity to "take leave" again and again and to cope with these partings, in whatever form they might appear. We must be able to mourn, and we must be able to deal with the constant leave-taking.

50

DREAMS AS GUIDES
DURING THE PROCESS OF MOURNING

Elena's dreams provided the impulse for the task of mourning, and the end of the dream series announced the end of a successful mourning process. I would like to discuss the references made in these dreams to the phases of mourning and bring them in line with the knowledge we have about mourning, provided above all by Bowlby and Parkes.[26] I would also like to examine the consequences for practical work with mourners.

A catastrophe announced itself in Elena's unconscious (the avalanche dream) which threatened to shake the very core of her existence. At first she experienced the dream as if she herself must die. This feeling was repeated in the dream of the calf that had to be slaughtered. The dream heralded a change in her life which would require all her strength. There was nevertheless an indication in this dream that there was a "sacred" dimension to the whole affair. Transcendence and meaning could be experienced, but this aspect only became really clear to her in her associations to the dreams. Death as catastrophe: that was the first thing that the unconscious had to say to Elena about the imminent death of the man she loved.

Dreams which depict the impending death of a loved one or the approaching end of a relationship as a "catastrophic situation" are common. As a further example I would like to include the dream of a forty-five year old man whose wife was suffering from cancer. Given her condition at the time, no one suspected that death was near.

He dreamt:

"I am in my garden. I am sitting at our garden table with

my wife, as usual. We are talking about something trivial. Then it grows quite dark. Before, the sun had been shining. It is alarmingly dark, as in the middle of the night. I can neither get my bearings nor find my wife again. I call out to her. She doesn't answer. I want to get a candle. I can't find the way any more – I no longer know where the entrance to the house is. I call for help. No one comes. I am desperate."

The man associated the darkness with the "end of the world," with the setting of the sun in the middle of the day. The following day, his wife died unexpectedly.

It seems to me important to plumb the depths of this catastrophic aspect when dealing with individuals who have suffered such a loss. We must try as far as possible to measure the extent of this loss. Someone who has suffered the loss of a loved one is only capable of doing this when he has come to terms with the death and no longer needs to defend himself against it. If we pay attention to this, it may be possible to help the individual who is about to lose someone he loves before the death actually occurs. Kübler-Ross[27] mentioned in the book, *Interviews with the Dying* (from which I have already quoted), that in the last phase – in which the person who is ill accepts death and perhaps just lies there peacefully, not wanting to be troubled with the problems of the world outside – it is those closest to him who need the most help. Assistance in this situation is limited to explaining to those who will be left behind the reason for the "detached" behavior of the dying person. They can be made to feel that someone shares the burden of what they are experiencing, knows what they are going through. When I discuss how one could best "help" the mourner in any given phase, I am not suggesting that the experience of death can be made painless. I mean only that individuals in this extreme situation don't feel completely alone, that they can come to terms with the situation better and therefore deal more effectively with the death event. There should be

52

no attempt to render the death experience innocuous through any sort of comforting gestures but the individual can be shown that he can cope with it. Those closest to the dying person must be shown how not to burden the last hours of the dying one with their own fears and troubles. If they don't feel completely alone in their desperation, it is easier for them to participate in the experience, which will in turn greatly influence the way in which they will perceive their own deaths. It is important that the helper appreciates just how great the shock that awaits the ones left behind will be.

The Phase of Denial

The first phase following the news of death was characterized, in Elena's case, by lack of feeling. Elena did not believe her partner had died. She herself felt dead and numbed.

In general, the first phase of mourning can be described in this way, and in cases of sudden death, this phase lasts somewhat longer. Bowlby[28] found that this phase may last anywhere from a few hours to about a week.

The helpers should be prepared in this phase to take care of the everyday errands and duties and also to take over a great many of the affairs surrounding the death. In this phase, it is important to let the mourner feel that he is not alone. On the other hand, he must not be declared unfit to manage his own affairs nor be completely monopolized. In interacting with the mourner it should always be remembered that, though he needs human warmth, he must continue to live an independent life amongst his friends and neighbors. It is important to find the right balance between being too close and being too distant, so that the mourner does feel that promises were made to him about the future which cannot be kept. For the mourner it is important that he can be as numb, as devoid of feeling as he is, and that no one reproaches him for his lack of tears. This paralysis does not spring from a lack of feeling, but rather from a shock to the feelings. The mourner is "paralyzed" by the single overwhelming emotion. The numbness which accompanies the phase of denial cannot, in my opinion, be seen only as a repression of the unpleasant news. It must be seen as a reaction to an emotion too overwhelming to be coped with. I consider the different outbreaks of emotion which occur in the course of the mourning process to be the unfolding of this one great initial emotion. It might be helpful if those assisting don't control their own emotions but weep instead, when they feel like weeping.

The sight of the deceased, the corpse, brings the loss more clearly to consciousness. If the deceased is not looked upon once again, we run the risk of replacing reality with our fantasy, of imagining that individuals still live on in some way, having perhaps only "gone away" on a journey. It is also essential that women who have given birth to a stillborn child, including premature births which do not survive, look at these infants once again, because otherwise they may imagine in future pregnancies that they are carrying something monstrous.

The Phase of Emotional Chaos

The phase of emotional chaos follows the phase of numbness: in Elena's case the emotions of fury, grief and joy. Bowlby[29] has also mentioned outbursts of anger in this connection and Parkes[30] mentions outbreaks of feelings of fear and restlessness. Although feelings of fear were less apparent in Elena's case, one still finds these feelings of fear with many mourners – for example, with the forty-five year old man who had dreamt of the "end of the world." He described the phase following the numbness thus:

"I had to snap out of the numbness, for there were still the children. I also had to take care of the obituary. But I

had such a terrible fear, I was afraid I could neither write
an obituary nor survive even a single day with the chil-
dren. I felt paralyzed by fear. I thought I could no longer
go on living. My twelve year old son took me by the
hand and said, 'But we're still here.'
This fear would return time and time again. Sometimes,
for no reason, I felt at the mercy of everyone and every-
thing. I would begin to grow cold – to shiver."

This man had been an anxious type even before the loss
of his wife. Elena, however, was no anxious woman but
tended to react with anger instead. It seems as if these emotional reactions that break out after the phase of numbness
correspond to the personality of the mourners. Of course,
the outbursts of anger and fury alternate with phases of
deep dejection.

The anger seems to be channeled in two directions.
Parkes and Bowlby[31] quote many instances where widows
accuse the doctors or even relatives of having failed to do
one thing or another. Only a small number of widows direct
their anger against the husband himself. The former seek in
their anger to find someone responsible for the death and
for their troubles. To have found him, even for a short time,
seems to lighten their burden. The others, who are angry at
their spouses, find the guilty party is the very person who
has abandoned them. This seems to me to be a more direct
form of anger than anger directed at the doctor. I have to
ask myself whether the anger directed at the doctor or the
hospital staff is not, then, a displaced anger, because one
doesn't dare to be angry with the deceased. Nevertheless it
was the deceased who left someone behind with many
difficult problems to solve. But perhaps the anger is simply
a reaction against the change in situation. After all, the
deceased has only in the rarest cases chosen death. In cases
of suicide, the anger of the next of kin is focused much
more directly on the deceased. But even the person who has
not 'chosen' death proves to those left behind how little was

required to turn their entire life situation upside down, how transitory, how fragile we humans are, how helpless in the face of this transitoriness. This reaction of fear, fury and powerlessness and the anger at this powerlessness will then be transferred directly onto the first one who crosses the path of the mourner. The search for a guilty party, if it is to be successful, must demonstrate and prove that we are not so powerless after all. It seems to me that it is our reaction to the powerlessness which we fear in ourselves and our own deaths that gives rise to this angry, furious or dejected behavior.

It is so difficult to admit to ourselves our helplessness in the face of death. When we get angry, when we search for a guilty party, often with remarkable energy, then we are pretending to ourselves that we are not so completely helpless. Perhaps this "game" even helps us to rally our forces to go on living. Perhaps we must permit ourselves this bit of deception. If finding a guilty party proves that this death was not an act of fate, but rather that someone had "just" made a mistake, then death would lose a bit of its cruelty. In that case, however, an individual would have to carry this burden.

Of course one doesn't have to go looking elsewhere for the guilty party; one can feel guilty about the death oneself. The outbreak of feelings of guilt is also part of this phase. Grof and Halifax[32] advance the theory that the length of the mourning process, and I would add to this the way of mourning, possibly even the "success" of the mourning, is essentially dependent upon the form of the conflicts between relatives and the deceased. They point out that guilt feelings were substantially less if the communication between those remaining behind and the dead had been good, if there had been a genuine leave-taking and if problems could still be discussed with one another. If guilt feelings were not too pronounced, the period of mourning was not prolonged indefinitely. The person who cannot work out his problems with the dying before death occurs will

56

certainly have to wrestle with his guilt feelings later on, with aggressions that still exist towards the deceased and now fall so strangely into emptiness. It is important to take such feelings of guilt very seriously in the therapy, as they express real problems which could not be sorted out as long as the partner was alive. Certainly it would be desirable, and it is clearly to be striven for that communication with the dying, that leave-taking is attended to with care.

Perhaps our ancestors understood better how to die. In literature[33] we are told again and again how the old father before his death wishes to speak to those closest to him. He straightens something out with one, gives another a piece of advice to guide him on his way, sometimes a word of concern, sometimes a word of recognition or tenderness, in which those generations perhaps indulged less than we do. We are told how the dying one meets one last time with his friends and his enemies, attempts to sort out disagreements – and then dies.

Massive outbreaks of anger, fury and guilt seem to occur more often in connection with individuals who die before their time[34] and who die suddenly. The death is then even more difficult to comprehend and cannot be assimilated. It is important for the helper to know that it is desirable for these emotions to emerge. It is more likely that these emotions will surface if one speaks about the deceased than if one "distracts" the mourner. Distraction can at times also be helpful, but in general it is a repression of the situation. The mourner cannot in any case evade his loss, so it is better to face the problem and speak about the dead. It also makes no sense to try to argue the mourner out of his feelings of guilt. As a helper one must simply take note of these guilt feelings without intensifying or reducing them. In a later phase, at least within the framework of therapy, the relationship problem that has caused and still causes guilt feelings must be worked upon. As a rule, many feelings of guilt disappear of their own accord and require no further therapeutic confrontation.

Elena said that the dream in which her letters were returned had also given her joy. It was joy in the fact that, instead of "nothing" remaining, in a certain sense the relationship still existed. One observes that mourners, along with anger, fury and grief, also experience repeatedly a deep feeling of joy in the simple fact that this relationship existed, that it is a piece of life that cannot be taken away from them, not even by death.

I think in this connection of a fifty-two year old woman who had suddenly lost her husband and had become severely depressed. She told me how it was when her husband had died. She told it in great detail. In a toneless voice she explained how superfluous she now felt, how shattered she was. But suddenly, her eyes lit up, and she said with animation, "We had a wonderful time together – he was such an interesting, good man! No one can take that away from me!" For a moment, she continued to smile dreamily. Then slowly, the shadow stole across her features again, and she said to me that she had lost so much; for that reason everything was now so worthless.

The joy over the stretch of life travelled together is as important a part of the mourning process as the problems and disagreements that there were. It is as wrong to consider only the conflicts as it is to look only at the harmonious aspects of the relationship.

The helper in this phase must expect that the fury, the anger of the mourner, will also be turned upon him, especially if he holds a different opinion on matters past or present. In this phase it is essential just to share in the experience of the mourner; this means really listening and really paying attention, and above all, not telling lengthy stories of one's own grief experiences.

Really productive mourning is being able to break the old pattern of relationship and allow a new pattern to form. There appears to be no other way for new potential in relationships and in life to be realized than by experiencing and enduring this emotional chaos. The emotional chaos is an

58

image of chaos in general, in which the old disappears and the new can take form.

The Phase of Search and Separation

Bowlby sees feelings of anger and guilt as aiding the search: as long as I can still get angry at someone, he is in some way still there. I understand the anger and the annoyance as meaning that the relationship has yet to be clarified. In the process of this the deceased will be sought and found once again, not merely as something which must ultimately be let go of, but rather as one's own relationship potential. It is a chance to see the deceased as an aspect of oneself. I see this searching not merely as a repression of the death, but rather as an attempt to integrate that which the deceased represented into the newly developing life structure.

But what form does this searching take? With Elena the searching could be seen in the dream about the scientific paper, which at first gave her the feeling that she had found George again. In doing what he would liked to have done, she searched for him and actually found him. Parkes[35] describes the way in which the London widows he questioned searched. With many mourners the search seems to have been a very real one. Parkes records a widow who always looked for the deceased in the supermarket; another always glanced toward her left side, because that was her husband's accustomed place. The fifty-two year old woman about whom I spoke always listened to the sound of cars. If she heard "the sound of her husband's car" she would become very nervous, wanting to rush out to the kitchen to make him something to eat. Only at this point would it dawn on her that this was absurd, that the sound of the car could have nothing at all to do with her husband any more. The forty-five year old man, who dreamt of the end of the world, searched unconsciously among all the women he saw for physical similarities to his wife. He realized that he would suddenly stare, fascinated, at a woman's hairstyle or at the line of her lips.

In general, places or activities which the deceased had once loved are the focus of attention. This can be taken so far that the mourner adopts the lifestyle of the deceased, even though it may not suit him at all. In this case, one is forced to view the search as an attempt to preserve the old familiar ways, as resistance against change. Nevertheless, I believe that the search can be a means of engaging repeatedly in an interaction with the person whom one has lost. The supposed finding plunges the mourner back into emotional chaos, precisely because he believes he has "found," and therefore must suffer again the pain of separation. This searching behavior seems to me to prepare the individual increasingly to accept the loss. It prepares him to continue living life without the deceased, while at the same time not giving up everything as lost. He experiences the intensity of the relationship as part of life. The searching and the separation throw the mourner back upon his own resources and make it clear that he must reclaim those characteristics and capabilities which he had delegated to the partner.

In this connection an eighty year old great grandfather told me that at Christmas time he had always "searched" for his wife near the toy store. That is where she would have been. Suddenly it was as if he heard her say, 'You old fool, now it is up to you to choose gifts for the great grandchildren!' He wanted to make clear to her that she had bought all the gifts for fifty-five years and that it was unthinkable for him to do this now. His wife just laughed and said, 'If you haven't learned by now, then it's high time you started!' And then he told me what an experience it had been for him to buy presents again for the first time since his boyhood. It had been difficult for him even to learn that one had to develop a feeling for the one for whom one wanted to buy a gift. It had been difficult for him to gain a sympathetic understanding of the wishes of someone else, and so forth.

60

The search often seems to express itself in the form of an inner dialogue. By means of this inner dialogue one finds the partner once again and can speak with him once more. For many mourners, especially for the older ones, it is very hard to have no one to talk to any more. The inner dialogue serves to replace the partner at first, offering at the same time the opportunity to interact with him once again. In most of the cases I have seen, this inner partner undergoes change with time, so that the mourner eventually has a new opposite number within him – scarcely comparable to the lost partner, but with whom he now interacts. So it seems to me to be possible by means of the inner dialogue to "find" the partner once again. The development of this dialogue leads then to the separation from the partner, as he once was. It must, however, be noted that it is also possible to cling to this inner dialogue, to repeat it over and over, to permit it no development. Then of course one does not take leave of this partner but rather in a mysterious way remains bound to him, with the result that no new relationships can develop in life.

The search occurs involuntarily. The process of mourning seems to me to have succeeded when the phase reflecting the need to separate and leave follows the "finding," and where this separation is accepted.

The repetition of this search-find-separate routine permits confrontation with the partner. It enables one to discover which part of oneself was bound up with the deceased partner. It is realized that the old conditions of life can no longer be counted upon and that one's own relationship to the world must be reconstructed.

In Elena's case this finding and separating was expressed particularly clearly in the dream of the border train station. Moreover, her psyche established here a clear limit: now she must let her loved one go. Even the searching behavior will help no further. In this dream it also became clear how very much a readiness to give up one's own life can also be bound to the search. This again in a double sense: firstly, in

61

the sense that one doesn't search for a way of continuing one's own life and is thus not oriented towards the future, clinging instead to the past and wanting to preserve the old habits; then in another, more concrete sense, one's own life no longer seems to be of value or the change demanded seems simply too great. Obviously in this phase of searching and separating, as in all phases of mourning, phases of despair, depression or apathy occur repeatedly, during which the mourner has the feeling that his life will never be the same, that it will never again be worth living. The thought of death occurs as a way out.

Bowlby notes that this phase of search and separation can last anywhere from weeks to years. In my experience, the intensity of the searching diminishes the more the mourner is able to express his chaotic emotions and the more he experiences "finding" not only as something external but as an internal finding of values that were hidden in the relationship. The values were part of his own potential and can become part of him now that the deceased no longer claims "ownership" of them.

In dealing with mourners in this phase it is important that one does not urge them to give up the "senseless" searching, thereby forcing them to accept the loss as final. It may certainly be suggested to those individuals who are still setting a place at the table two years after the death, that perhaps the search should be carried out in a different way. It is a burden for the helpers to hear the same stories about the deceased, but this is also a form of searching and finding. Naturally it is also tiresome to listen over and over again to the fantasizing about where the dead one, who is not "really dead," could be. A common fantasy is, for example, that some secret service or other has abducted the individual, having laid a substitute body to rest in his place, or that a distant lover has managed to abduct the spouse. These fantasies occur more frequently in the case of a sudden death. Especially lively are the fantasies surrounding those missing in acting during a war. Since in this situation it really cannot

62

be ascertained for certain whether the missing person is dead or not, it is difficult to put an end to the fantasy. By means of these fantasies the link with the person who is missing is maintained, so that should he never come back, separation cannot take place until much later, if at all. For the mourner, it is important that he can tell his stories and speak repeatedly of his fantasies because, in this way, emotions are kept awake.

The Phase of New Relationship to Oneself and the World

When the search and separation phase reaches the stage where it doesn't occupy every thought and fill the mind of the mourner, then the next phase of relating in a new way to oneself and the environment can begin. The pre-condition for this is that the deceased has become an "inner figure." Either the mourner experiences the deceased as a sort of inner companion who may also undergo change, or he feels that a great deal that was formerly lived out in the relationship has now become part of his own potential. In Elena's case the transition to this new phase was seen in the dream in which George rose from his coffin, and she experienced resurrection with him. George becomes her companion once again, but in a completely different way, and a great many new contacts, new friends, are found. Thus the initial phase of mourning is completed. The better the mourner adjusts to the new roles which life demands of him and the more able he is to see what characteristics he can develop as an individual within these new roles, the sooner he regains his self-confidence and self-respect. In this phase he can then dispense with those who previously looked after him. These helpers may even become an obstacle in his way if they don't accept the new independence and the change in the mourner, preferring to see him helpless in order to pre-serve their role. A successful mourning process requires that the mourner undergo change and accordingly form new relationships.

Seeing the deceased as an inner figure, as an inner guide, can nevertheless also have very peculiar, unhealthy consequences. For example, the personality of the mourner may simply slip into the role of the deceased, doing what the deceased did, thinking what the deceased thought, becoming involved where the deceased would have been involved, thus not really seeing one's own options and wishes. The deceased settles upon the mourner like a second personality. Naturally it is then not possible to create a new relationship to oneself and one's surroundings. The integration of potentialities that were represented by the deceased and which can be recognized as one's own must always be considered in the light of one's own personality to see if they really are suitable.

A new relationship to oneself and the world is also seen in the fact that the loss is now accepted, that many life patterns that had become habitual in relationship to the deceased are now set aside and new life patterns take their place. This occurs without the deceased simply being forgotten.

In this phase also, relapses into phases of mourning already passed through are to be expected. This is due to self-doubt which arises when the euphoria that is often associated with the new phase of relatedness to oneself and the environment begins to fade. The man who dreamt of the end of the world when his wife died experienced a distinctly euphoric phase after he had confronted his chaotic emotions and given a great deal of thought to the patterns of relationship that had existed between them. He had become far more conscious of his own traits and his own potential in the area of relationships. He cultivated relationships which he had had no chance to cultivate previously, as his wife was jealous of everything he undertook outside the marriage. Now he felt very good about this. He had entered into an affectionate relationship with a woman who, however, doubted that they could build up a stable relationship with one another. The euphoric state collapsed at this point. He felt that he was once again experiencing a great loss. He did not accept the woman's reservations as justified, as something that one could talk about, but rather as a clear rejection, and thus fell once again into chaotic grief and had to go through all the phases of mourning again. It appears that individuals who have lost a loved one react very strongly for a long period of time to any sort of loss. They suffer a sort of relapse and must then go through the entire process of mourning once again. However, in most cases, this is not experienced with the original intensity.

Brown, Harris and Copeland[36] indicate that individuals who have lost their mother before the eleventh year of life show a distinct tendency later in life to react far more violently than others to loss experiences. We will come back to this observation later on. When someone has lost someone who meant a great deal to them, they will react far more strongly to loss and separation than someone who has never experienced loss. Still, the experience of death is an intense emotional experience and burden; Parkes[37] speaks of this as being the most severe stress that can befall an individual.

Experiences characterized by strong emotions tend to be recalled in similar situations, such that the new situation tends to be falsified by the "old" one. One behaves in the same way as during the earlier emotional stress experience and re-experiences the same emotions. If the emotion is endured and the programmed ways of reacting revealed as such and halted, then the "compulsion to repeat" will gradually become weaker. This is true in dealing with any powerful complex,[38] but it is especially relevant in dealing with a death experience. For this reason it is important that the mourner as well as those around the mourner know that "relapses" are bound to occur. It helps to understand that the relapses are not actually relapses, but represent recurring opportunities to assimilate loss experiences in general and in particular the one great loss.

This becomes very pronounced when an individual loses someone else within a few years of the first loss. During the mourning process the two losses then become entangled. With every new experience of death it seems as if one is losing all those individuals whom one has already lost all over again. It does help, however, to know that one has successfully withstood the task of mourning once already. One remembers the way it was and is possibly not quite so desperate as the first time. The phase in which the mourner is convinced he cannot survive this loss is usually much shorter. The mourner "knows" that he has already survived loss once. It is far more difficult for someone who repressed the task of mourning the first time around to deal with a new loss. In most cases he falls into a deep depression. More will be said about this later.

Elena's dream of a medicinal bath can be seen as the conclusion of the mourning process. By "conclusion" it is not implied that Elena could not fall into mourning again, that she would not react more emotionally to separation than she did before the loss. By "conclusion" it is understood that Elena felt for the first time that her love of life had returned, in spite of death. New relationships could be entered into, even though death may be lying in wait round every corner.

Death confronts us in a radical way with the question of meaning. For Elena, it was obviously not enough that she was able to integrate the relationship with George as far as possible into her own personality. It was not enough that she could continue a life with new options and a new self-awareness in which a consciousness of death had found its place. She needed also to be able to experience that life – even in the face of death – had a meaning. The dream represented this realization of meaning as something which came to her after she had been healed in the bath.

Among others in mourning I have observed that the sense of meaning can be rediscovered when a new relationship to themselves and the world has really developed. It could be experienced once they became aware of the fact that the death of the mourned one not only took a great deal away from them, but had also brought them a great deal. This occurs in a very late phase of a successful mourning period, and one should not deceive oneself about the pain, the desperation, the exhaustion, the disruption and the lack of physical contact that the death of a loved one brings with it.

In order to be able to mourn properly, to be able to assimilate the loss, the mourner as well as those around him must be ready to accept death and mourning. The dreadful despair must be accepted as such and must be regarded as appropriate to this particular life situation. In addition, the chaotic emotions, especially the anger, must be endured. This is made easier by an understanding that this emotional chaos represents the dismantling of the old patterns of relationship and the old habits and therefore also the creation of a new potential. It is also very important that everything connected with the death is talked about rather than hushed up, even if this seems strange at times.

Reminiscing about experiences shared with the deceased is important in order that the relationship remains meaningful to the bereaved, and the process of integration in his own psyche can succeed. Elena's dream series as presented here shows how essential dreams are in coping with loss, how they can even steer the process of mourning. Jung's theory about the self-regulation of the psyche seems to be correct.[39] The unconscious provides those impulses which are necessary to the continuation of life. Elena's dream series is not an isolated one. I know of several dream series that led into the essential phases of mourning in the same way. Most of these dreams were very easy to interpret.

The phase of searching, finding and separating, in particular, occupied an important place among the dreams. All authors who mention such dreams state the importance of this phase, in which one often meets again with the deceased, who seems to be "alive" and even healthy. The

67

dreamer is aware, however, that he is dealing with someone who has died and knows also that they must part again.[40]

A good example of this seems to me to be the dream of a seventy-eight year old man who had lost his wife a month previously. Originally he had planned to follow her into death. He felt they had experienced so much with one another that it was fitting they also die together. But shortly after his wife's death, he had a dream in which she appeared to him more full of life than she had been for a long time. She said to him, 'I can always come to you, but don't do anything rash when you want to come to me.' This dream comforted him a great deal, and although he sensed the distance between himself and his wife, it was still a meaningful distance. This man was of the sort who never put much value on his dreams. But in the light of his loss his dreams had become very important to him; he waited every night for the meeting with his wife, and she would give him "help with life." I believe one cannot express this any better: dreams can, in these situations, provide help with life. They need not be only comforting. For many it might be very painful when the loved one appears, only to withdraw again; still, this pain serves to prepare one for the continuation of life. It is not only important that the dreamer be comforted: it is still more important that he come to terms with the new conditions of life. The dreams in this phase tend to be lively and realistic. Their meaning is immediately clear, even to those who don't know much about symbolic interpretation.

Self-help groups of mourners, such as exist in England,[41] seem to be very well suited to keeping the process of mourning moving in a positive way. Individuals who share a similar life situation can be of great assistance to one another. At the very least, they can be a stimulant to the expression of emotion. Nevertheless, the transformation, the enduring of the transformation, must be borne alone. The supporting power of others also has its limits.

WHEN MOURNING
IS PROLONGED OR REPRESSED

Each of the phases of mourning carries the danger that one comes to a standstill in it, that one chooses the way back and no longer confronts mourning as an ongoing process. In therapy we often have to deal with individuals who have at some point in their lives lost someone who was very close to them and did not mourn sufficiently. In our society it is often regarded as a sign of strength when one succeeds in overcoming grief very quickly. This repression of mourning can lead to depressions which are a mystery to the person affected. Looking into these depressions, one frequently finds incomplete mourning processes and repressed grief. Another death event, even one involving someone less close, the reaching of the same age as the deceased, the anniversary of the death, in short, any situation intimately connected with the deceased, can trigger this type of depression.

Freud saw the connection between mourning and melancholy,[42] in that they resemble one another in appearance and both follow the loss of a loved object. Freud described mourning as a normal reaction, melancholy as pathological. The difference between mourning and melancholy lay in the fact that the mourner knew *what* he had lost, whereas the melancholic knew *whom* he had lost, but not *what;* thus, the object-loss is partly lost to consciousness.[43] Apart from this there is a difference, according to Freud, in that in mourning, the relationship to the object is an uncomplicated one – whereas in melancholy, there exists an ambivalent conflict: love and hate towards the lost object exist simultaneously.

Jacobson[44] regretted that, by Freud's lumping together

69

of mourning and melancholy, the depressive mood would be regarded as basically pathological. She was of the opinion that depressive states of mind can also develop as a normal mood and need not necessarily be pathological. We do not label every elevated mood pathological. However, depressive conditions also develop, in Jacobson's opinion, "from aggressive tensions and are for this reason an expression of a conflict situation, a neurotic or psychotic conflict, or a conflict with reality."[45] Moods of this type contain within themselves a pathological potential; that is, the depression can become pathological if regressive processes are set in motion, or if severe problems which have not yet been overcome play a part in the conflict. This opinion of Jacobson's seems to me to be valid. It corresponds to my own observation of depressive individuals.

Mourning can have a depressive undertone when hostility and aggressive feelings towards the deceased still exist, yet cannot be admitted.

Anger plays a part in every mourning process. It is anger because one has been abandoned, and anger at the fact that one is forced to come to terms with the loss and make new arrangements in order to get on with life. Apart from this, the relationship which one had with the deceased must be reappraised, and it is therefore to be expected that aggressive feelings must emerge. There is, on the other hand, the maxim that evil should not be spoken of the dead, and so these aggressive feelings must be repressed. If this happens, however, the process of mourning comes to a standstill, and the potential for depressive reactions is created. The more severe the loss experience, the more the aggressions bound up with it have been repressed, the more undealt-with conflicts there are, and the less an ego is in a position to endure conflict, the more pathological these reactions will be.

With the help of examples taken from my therapeutic practice, I would like to discuss the problems of the repressed and prolonged mourning process.

70

Problems in the Phase of Denial

If this phase is prolonged, then we have before
individual who has repressed the loss and thus the great
emotion connected with it. These individuals behave as if
nothing had happened. The loss of a loved one cannot,
however, be completely repressed. A favorite form of
escape is "keeping busy."

*A forty year old business woman, who had lost her hus-
band in an accident, said, "If he isn't here any more, then
I must look after things." She allowed herself no sign of
weakness; she told her children that their father would
certainly be disappointed in them if they were weak now,
if they were to cry. He would expect them to be brave,
like soldiers. The whole family came across as very
heroic in the way they carried on father's work, and they
were admired by all and sundry, who couldn't sing their
praises loud enough. But in time, the affair did not seem
quite so heroic. Those in their immediate circle had come
to take the family's bravery for granted; also, the memory of the deceased slowly faded. Then the woman
began to seek out doctors with an assortment of psychosomatic complaints. The doctors sent her into psychotherapy. She described her life and noted with pride
how she had coped with the loss of her husband:
"Everything went on as if he were still there – nothing
changed at all!" Astonished, I asked, "Nothing at all?"
To this she responded, after a little thought, that it had
certainly been difficult, running the whole business
without any kind of support. It had also been hard never
feeling any kind of tenderness any more; but the good
feeling that she was able to keep everything in order,
even without him, made up for this – for she had continued to run things and was able to raise the children without their father. The problem was just that now it worried
her that her body was no longer cooperating. In answer*

71

to my question, about how she felt otherwise, she said that she was no longer accustomed to feeling: she ful-filled her duties every day, and this gave her a good feeling.

This woman had been able to circumvent the blow dealt to her self-perception and her attitude toward life in that she simply immersed herself in the work of her deceased husband: his life and her life had merged. She had never consciously experienced the grief connected with the loss. In answer to my question (about whether she had missed her husband from time to time), she replied that she had, of course, but whenever she had missed him, she had worked even harder for his business.

It was difficult to make the woman see that her psychosomatic difficulties, especially her heart symptoms, could quite possibly have something to do with the loss of her husband. She felt all that was long since over and done with. It was four years after the death when the woman was referred to psychotherapy; it should have been much sooner. However, she declared herself willing to confront the death of her husband, if that would help. I asked her to bring photographs from the years they had shared together. She did this, began to talk about him, began to recall different things, and with time could recover the experience of grief. She also soon realized that she had of course also had a great deal of difficulty with him and that, in spite of this, she desperately wished in her loneliness that he were with her again. Only after a very long phase, during which the memories of her husband were reformed, did she begin to dream. The first dream she remembered was:

"A corpse in a coffin is sent all over the world. No one knows to whom the corpse belongs. No one wants anything to do with it. I see the coffin and remember that my husband's coffin was very similar to it. I give instructions that the coffin be buried."

The woman now acknowledges to herself that her husband has died, and she takes it upon herself to look after his burial, so that the problem is laid to rest. The dream shows very clearly that this dead man, even if she was not thinking about him, was still very much in existence and was sent throughout the entire world.

The dream motif of an unburied corpse which is suddenly discovered is a common one. These dreams need not necessarily mean that we do not wish to acknowledge the death of an individual. They may just as well have to do with the fact that something within ourselves is lifeless, has perhaps even died, and we have also overlooked the process of burial and mourning. Though mourning is demanded most radically when we have lost someone we loved – since, in this situation, our perception of ourselves and our environment is most deeply shaken – it is also required when we lose something that was an extremely important part of ourselves.

In 1937 Helene Deutsch[46] was the first to describe four patients who had lost someone in childhood and had not mourned. They suffered later from depressive phases as well as other difficulties in life. Only in the course of therapy did it become apparent that the reason for this lay in childhood losses which had not been mourned. In each case the feelings associated with the loss event had not been integrated. According to Deutsch, this observation was confirmed repeatedly by many therapists. The loss need not necessarily have taken place during childhood; it could just as well have taken place during the adult years.[47] Individuals who bypass conscious mourning will always be described as self-assured individuals who are proud of their independence and self-control. They are disinclined to express their emotions, view tears as an unseemly weakness and go on living after a loss as if nothing had happened. This description, in which Bowlby supports Deutsch, Volkan and others, confirms my own observations. These individuals reject all memories of the deceased and want no mention made of them, or if something must be said, then only if it is simultaneously stressed how well they are dealing with the loss. Bowlby[48] states further that this type of individual often has a tendency towards psychosomatic illness, especially headaches and sleeplessness, in extreme cases, even excessive drinking. Bowlby stressed that many factors can lead to a diverting of grief. It seems established, however, that it is precisely the very "brave" individual who represses his grief that will be overcome by it, probably in the form of depression or low spirits, which perhaps don't quite deserve to be termed "depression."

It also seems to me important to consider the role that the loss of an unborn child plays in the lives of women (and men!):

A thirty-six year old man sought me out because he suffered from frequent insomnia, and apart from that, felt in low spirits. He said there was no apparent reason for this – he had a suitable job that gave him pleasure, his marriage was good, he loved his wife and his two children, his youth had been uneventful – and all this seemed to be true. I asked him if he had at some point perhaps lost grandparents whom he had loved very much. But this was not the case; his grandparents were still alive at a ripe old age. His parents were also still alive. He had never lost anyone. As he said this, he hesitated a little and then added that his wife in fact had had a miscarriage about two years previously; she had lost a child in the third month of pregnancy. He had looked forward to the child very much, but they already had two healthy children, and anyway, an embryo like that isn't really a human being yet ... As he gained insight into just how much this child meant to him, how he had looked forward to it with so much joy, it became clear to him that the miscarriage really had also been an emotional loss that should and must be mourned.

A great difficulty seems to me to lie in the fact that we have our own ideas about when we are permitted to mourn and when not, and how long mourning is appropriate. This man said at first, "One can't mourn an embryo as one would someone with whom one has lived for a long time." This seems obvious, but when one considers how important this embryo was for the man, what fantasies were already connected with it, how his life had already begun to include this embryo, then his statement is not to be taken at face value. There are no fixed rules as to how long and for what or for whom we need to mourn: the more emotionally bound we are to someone or something, the more we will have to mourn.

A further example involving an unmourned embryo:

A thirty-eight year old woman sought out therapy because she always felt tired and no doctor could find out why. She was married and childless. She indicated that she and her husband did not want to bring any children into the world and that, apart from this, she found children a nuisance and costly. In the course of our discussion we got around to the fact that she had once aborted a pregnancy. She mentioned it, as that day was the anniversary of the abortion, and by coincidence she had a session with me. She mentioned it very casually; it struck me that she mentioned it at all and that she had noted the exact day. She explained how glad she had been that the child had been "done away with." I said, just as casually, that sometimes one had mixed feelings about a situation. She warded this off, maintained that she had just been glad, and that she had never even felt guilty. In the next session she told me that she had been very angry with me the last time: I had tried to convince her that she had guilt feelings about her abortion. She didn't want to talk about it any more, and instead she brought up a current problem which she said was urgent. Approximately two months later in a therapy session she suddenly began to

75

weep and said that she had looked forward so much to the child that was growing in her body. Suddenly she had experienced herself as a fertile field, which was a feeling about her body quite different to the one she had had before. She felt completely differently about herself as an individual and as a woman. But still, she could not go back on her decision to terminate the pregnancy, quite apart from the fact that she really had the feeling that she would have been "an impossible mother."

One can see also in the case of this woman that she didn't realize what the abortion had meant for her, namely the loss of something that she had felt was essential in her life, as she herself expressed it in her image of the "fertile field." In deciding to abort she had decided not to permit this field to become fertile. Whether she decided rightly or wrongly is not the issue, but she had to see that it was for her a loss and must be mourned. In addition, she had to come to terms with the aggressive feelings associated with this event. She was angry at the "child" who had put her in the position of having to kill it. After these aggressive feelings became accessible to her, she could admit her guilt feelings and accept them as appropriate.

Denial can also take the form of involving oneself with another person who has suffered a loss, with the result that one only indirectly attends to one's own mourning duties. A minister told me that it was his strength to accompany others in their pain, others who had lost someone. This minister had himself lost his wife a few years previously. He said, "As long as I can occupy myself with others who have lost someone, everything is all right. When these individuals don't need me any more, then I become sad myself; then I think of my own wife. But I am not allowed to be sad, because I know that she is waiting for me in heaven."

This minister, who helps so many in their mourning, does not permit mourning in his own case because he does not need to be sad if his wife is with God.

It seems to me that this represents another problem: there are individuals who, on the basis of their philosophy of life, believe that they are not permitted to mourn. They overlook the fact that, as the bereaved, they have nevertheless suffered a great loss which affects their entire life.

What this minister himself had observed – that he felt well as long as he could support others in mourning – stands to reason: as long as he could accompany others in their mourning, he could identify with it. When they didn't need him any more, he himself had to mourn, and he was not permitted to do that. The danger with individuals who mourn vicariously, and this opportunity presents itself particularly in the helping professions, is that they then break down when there is no one whom they can support in their grief. It is, of course, also possible that they "mother" the other person too much in this vicarious mourning and thus hinder them in independently restructuring their lives. Vicarious mourning can be understood in this way: that one can project onto others the aspects of oneself that urgently need the mourning process, and in doing so, one gives away the help that one needs oneself. This behavior option is of course always available to us, not only when mourning is to be carried out.[49] With mourning in particular this opportunity presents itself because the helper who has also lost someone is especially well accepted, since he of course understands how the other is feeling.

Another form of stalling in the phase of denial reveals itself in that individuals speak of the great "emptiness" they have felt in themselves since the death. This emptiness cannot be filled by anything; they live like automatons. Szonn, in his essay describing the mourning process guided by associations with given images,[50] mentioned the case of a mother who unintentionally had run over her daughter with a tractor. As a result she suffered from depression, especially in autumn, because her daughter had died in the autumn. This woman herself said that she had not been able to mourn; she had felt empty. She sought counseling because her relationship to her second child had now begun to suffer. Szonn describes how he first gave the woman the motif "brook" to picture, and in the second session the motif "the path to the grave." At this the woman began to weep, and this weeping appears to have signaled the onset of mourning. The article was unfortunately so short that it is difficult to see what really happened. Szonn stated that, in a few sessions of guided image association, the depression was significantly alleviated. In my opinion this really happened because the mourning process was set in motion.

It appears to me that this type of image association can be very helpful in triggering the neglected mourning process, especially in cases where the individual experiences himself as "empty."

Problems in the Phase of Emotional Chaos

It is possible to see all the problems discussed so far as representing attempts to avoid moving on into the phase in which emotions surface. Individuals who get stuck in the second phase of the mourning process basically make a different impression, and are in a completely different stage of the process, than those who come to a halt in the first phase. Those who get stuck in the first phase are individuals who want to avoid mourning altogether. Those who come to a standstill in a later phase are those individuals who don't find their way out of mourning. They become chronic mourners. They also appear to be depressed, not because they have repressed the pain, but because they are overwhelmed by it, absorbed by it. They are compelled always to think about it and no longer know how to carry on. Upon looking closer, one observes that in some way they also block the process of mourning, and do not submit to this process of transformation, even though it appears as if they are completely involved in it.

John is nineteen. Two years ago he lost his father; he is the oldest of three children and has unexpectedly become head of the family. His mother has become accustomed to asking him the questions that she used to ask his father. John is still in school, facing his final examinations, and has enormous difficulty concentrating. He thinks this is because he can't sleep. Up until the death of the father he had been a very good student. Since then, his achievement level has fallen off. Immediately following the death, the teachers had been lenient with him. Now they are no longer lenient, finding him too despondent. He should slowly be getting over this loss. A minister to whom he went for advice sent him into therapy.

When I asked how he had experienced the death of his father, he told me that his father had been sick for a long time and this had hung over the whole family like a shadow. They had actually all been quite glad when the father died. He had had a good relationship with the father, and especially towards the end, they had had many good talks with each other. The father also had asked him to take over his place in the family. John had done this willingly and had enjoyed it, but he felt the burden was too much for him; he could hardly do anything at all with his friends any more..

All that sounded very reasonable. John spoke with little modulation in his voice, made a very serious impression, seeming much older than he was. This is one example of how the life of an individual can change through the death of someone close. Then the school boy suddenly finds himself "head of the family" and justifiably feels overburdened.

That was one aspect of his problem. Another was that he never expressed his anger about the death of his father. John remarked that, since the death of his father, he had had some strange dreams. In these dreams he was always very angry that the father had died and reproached him for it.

I asked him how the family had reacted to the death. As is usual with a long illness, a great deal of mourning was done in advance. Parkes calls this anticipatory mourning "worry work."[51] Human beings try to prepare for major changes in that they try to imagine how it will be. But this anticipatory mourning does not replace the mourning process. Imagining the final absence is something entirely different from the real absence, which is radical and merciless and cannot be anticipated in fantasy. In John's family some things concerning the impending death were worked out while the father was still alive. The father himself appeared to have carried out a process of leave-taking, both from life and from his family, during the course of which there had been weeping and mourning. Nevertheless, as far as this preparatory grieving was concerned, anger was never expressed. I then asked John whether he had ever been angry at fate. He said that of course he had been angry; he had also lost his girlfriend because he could not spend time with her any more, but there was no point in being angry when one had been "struck down by fate." I attempted to make clear to him that it was entirely natural to be angry about these things. It was natural to be angry that he was now so overburdened, in spite of all the love he felt for his father, in spite of the sympathy for his father that his life couldn't end the way he would have wished it. I also spoke to him about the fact that one could also be angry that someone had to suffer as much as his father had suffered, that one could become very confused about life by something like this.

I asked John to try to remember as many of the "anger dreams" as he could. He did this, wrote them down, then brought his brother to the therapy sessions so that, together, they could act out these anger dreams. John had correctly recognized that anger had been excluded from his mourning process and also that the father had been extremely idealized

80

by the mother. The children had taken over this idealization, although they naturally had had other sorts of experiences with their father, too. John gradually realized that the father had been very egoistic, even before the onset of his illness, and that the children had suffered a great deal as a result of this egoism. In retrospect, John was very angry about this. After nine such "anger sessions," John reported that he could sleep much better, that he wasn't so afraid of sleeping as he had been and, above all, he didn't have so many outbursts of anger as previously. At this point he mentioned for the first time that he had "gone up in smoke" over the smallest thing and that his mother had been very worried about this change in him. No wonder, the anger was there, but not only anger – also fear. Because the anger had to be repressed, it always burst out when John felt overburdened. Naturally he felt overburdened quite often, not only because of the very real external demands, but also because he was not permitted to express his anger, his annoyance and thus could never come to terms with the less pleasant aspects of his father.

A fear of death apparently also hid behind the anger. Why else should he have been afraid of sleep if he didn't associate this nightly sinking into sleep with the possibility of never waking up again? John's sense of security in life was deeply and negatively affected by the illness and death of his father. He was made painfully aware that the human being is mortal. In addition, the parents dealt with the illness of the father as a "blow of fate" and simply accepted it without protest. This attitude isn't valid for an eighteen year old youth; he must be able to rebel against death, so that he can find the courage to live again.

"Eternal" Guilt Feelings

Guilt feelings are bound to arise as part of a mourning process following the normal course. Who can really claim to have participated in a relationship without default? In the face of a death, feelings of guilt take on a radical, even brutal significance: no further discussion can clear the air, one can no longer make amends. All theoretical efforts to make amends founder on the fact that the deceased is no longer there. Certainly one can try to become aware of the sources of guilt and try, where possible, to avoid the same mistakes in other relationships. But guilt feelings cannot be avoided, and, if someone dies towards whom we feel guilt, then we become aware of what this means existentially: to be a human being who must feel guilty but deludes himself nevertheless into thinking he can avoid it.

In my practice I often have to deal with guilt feelings towards the deceased. Either those seeking advice don't know any more which way to turn out of sheer guilt, or the guilt feelings are repressed, but though dormant, are still exerting a negative influence on the psyche.

In my opinion guilt feelings are closely connected to something that was never worked out in the relationship between two individuals. They relate to the ideal which one had imagined with respect to the relationship to the deceased and the extent to which this ideal measured up to the reality. There are individuals who have made an effort to define their relationship and who – this, to me, is the important point – have admitted how much they remain indebted to each other in spite of all efforts. These people have also admitted to themselves that their efforts also have their limits. With such individuals I have always observed that their guilt feelings never get out of hand and concern things that do not strike at the core of their existence.

A man whose wife suffered from cancer for many long years used the time to speak with her a great deal about the thirty-year partnership they had shared. They relived pleasures, and discussed disappointments once again, though this was difficult for them both. He said a few weeks after the death of his wife that he was very thankful for the many long talks that they were able to have together. The only guilty feeling that he had was that he had not fulfilled her wish that he stay the night with her in the hospital, because he didn't want to face the argument with the hospital staff. He thinks now a great deal about this and would gladly make amends if he could.

This feeling of guilt is of a completely different quality from the guilt feelings of a fifty-five year old man, who sought out therapy because of severe depression.

He told me in the first hour that he had lost his wife five years ago, and since then, he suffered continuously from feelings of guilt. Then he looked at me searchingly and said, "Dr. X, the psychiatrist who referred me, felt that the guilt was unfounded, but that's not true." And then he spoke of how unloving he had been to his wife, that he had treated her like a household servant who had occasionally to put in a public appearance. He never showed her affection and had continuously thrown in her face the fact that she wouldn't fulfill her marital duties. He told her she was good for nothing, although she was good for a great deal. He was certain that his behavior had driven her to her grave. This became horrifyingly clear to him one week after the funeral. He realized what he had lost, and that it was too late to change things. He asked his grown-up children if it were true that he had been so impossible with their mother. The children confirmed it. From that point onwards, he felt driven from place to place. He didn't have a peaceful moment; he felt miserable, and guilty, simply guilty. He had been to a pastor who tried to comfort him, but he was inconsolable. He considered whether it wouldn't be for the best if he killed himself, because to carry around such a burden of guilt was terrible. But he didn't want to commit suicide either, because then his children would have not only a brutal man but also a suicide case as a father, apart from which he didn't have the courage to do it. He had already held a pistol to his head on one occasion, but

he was a coward. If he had committed a murder, then he could at least be in prison, but he had only committed psychological murder, for which he could not atone.
He said that he always had the same dream: he stands in front of his house and looks for his wife. He calls her, but she does not come.

I told this man that I couldn't take his guilt feelings away from him; I could only try to clarify the relationship he had had with his wife. It was possible that in the process of this clarification his guilt feelings would diminish. He accepted my statement that I couldn't take away his burden of guilt. He was willing to consider my ideas seriously, to work with his dreams and to attempt to shed some light on the relationship he had shared with his wife. He maintained that he really didn't know very much about this relationship any more. In that, he was very wrong indeed. Xaver had been plagued by a great many feelings of guilt even while his wife was still alive. He had had a fine sense for the psychological forces that were at work in his surroundings, but he had always managed to lay the blame on his wife, to project the blame onto her. The moment his wife was no longer there, the entire burden of guilt fell back onto him. In addition, he burdened himself with the guilt that could justifiably be attributed to his wife. It is not possible that, in a relationship, one partner alone is guilty.

I induced him to tell the entire story of his marriage. He had no dreams at this point, except the one in which he continually searched for his wife and could not find her. While he told the story of his marriage, we attempted to understand the problems which had, of course, always existed. As a result it became clear to him that many of his unloving actions were reactions to an unnerving habit of his wife's that repeatedly made him feel insecure. Nothing at all would ever be discussed between them. For this reason I suggested that he create an image as he relived all these memories of his wife and "speak" with his wife as if she were still alive. He found this childish, but did it neverthe-less, often taking over the role of his wife. In this way his wife became more and more lifelike in his memories, and the relationship was worked upon. He could also see that his wife wasn't the angel that, since her death, he held her to be. Nor was she the witch that he had believed her to be while she lived. He no longer saw himself only as a failure; he saw that he had neglected a great deal and was guilty of a great deal within the relationship, but he also saw that he was not the only guilty one. When we began to discuss the memories of his wife's sickness, after thirty-two therapy sessions, he began to carry out anticipatory mourning. When he described her death, he began to grieve as if his wife had died at that point in time. A phase of intensive confrontation with his wife in the "Hereafter" set in. He began to idealize this fantasy relationship that they now had, even began to send love letters to her in the next world – and I was more and more at a loss as to what to do with this symbiotic phase. Apparently he still had a need to idealize their relationship and even to put loving feelings to the test. In the past, if he for once had felt a little bit "romantic," his wife went out of her way to let him know that he shouldn't act like an old lady. He now enjoyed living out his tender side and his romantic inclinations with this fantasy image of his wife. This idealized fantasy relationship lasted about four months. Then he remarked that his wife was changing more and more in his fantasy; she took on more and more of his own characteristics, which really puzzled him. I indi-cated to him that this was an essential development in the process of mourning and told him that this feeling experi-ence had become a part of his own potential. The mourning process was completed, and he could go on living now with this new potential.

He took up a relationship with a neighbor that gave both of them a great deal of pleasure. He visited me thereafter once every year and told me how he was coping with his guilt feelings. He was very impressed by the fact that he still felt so guilty, even though he could see the extent of his own guilt more realistically and was now quite capable of accepting this guilt as his. Working on his relationship to his deceased wife had enabled him to see these guilt feelings in relative terms.

It seemed to me to be important in the treatment of this man never to attempt to comfort him or to see his guilt feelings from my perspective, but rather to let him attempt to discover where the guilt really lay. Often during treatment I had wished that he were a practicing Christian, so that he could confess and believe in absolution, but this option was not available to him. Individuals who come into therapy as a result of a death and with attendant feelings of guilt often cannot believe in forgiveness.

The problem arises when the emotional chaos associated with grief cannot be experienced to the full. When emotional storms break over the mourner again and again – certain aspects of which must be denied (anger, for example, but guilt feelings as well) – these mourners then seem to become stuck in this phase. They often reach for medication because the emotional chaos becomes unbearable.[52]

But guilt feelings alone can imprison the mourner in this phase, even when not repressed. Guilt feelings are apparently capable of disturbing the individual's self-perception to such an extent that he simply cannot see how life can continue. When guilt feelings are this pronounced, these mourners need outside help. I agree with Parkes that, in such cases, medication can alleviate the sleep disturbances, but cannot solve the problem. If mourning really is the process in which the behavior which existed in the relationship to a loved one must be analyzed, then the guilt feelings that are associated with the relationship, and also represent behavior patterns, should also be worked upon and resolved. This is important even though it is at first painful and can shake the individual to his very core.

Just how far such guilt feelings are to be interpreted as disguised death wishes aimed at the partner while he was still alive is questionable. In the case of Xaver they could be interpreted in this way. Nevertheless, it should also be noted that death wishes are not necessarily to be interpreted as meaning that the partner literally should die. Death wishes could also mean that the relationship, as it exists, must be altered. This can be seen in very symbiotic partners in particular. Quite apart from death wishes, guilt feelings form part of a partnership, because we can never realize our idea of an ideal relationship, and for this reason, are always "guilty."

It has been my experience that guilt feelings in a mourning process are not only connected with the fact that the relationship to the deceased was unclarified. They can just as well indicate that much that should have been lived in one's own life was not lived in this relationship. These guilt feelings are then seen exclusively in connection with the deceased. It is not just a question of possibilities which weren't explored in the relationship to the deceased, but of the "unlived life" as it really pertains to one's own life. It nevertheless appears to some that they could pinpoint what they have missed by seeing it in connection with guilt feelings related to the deceased. In this way, of course, they also express symbolically that it is past and gone forever.

This was particularly evident to me in the case of an analysand whose analyst had killed himself.[53] This analysand developed very strong guilt feelings; she felt responsible for this suicide, solely responsible. Certainly a bit of heroics and hero fantasy played a role in this, even if it was "negative heroism." Because she had depended so much on the transference to this man, she was extremely threatened by his death and had to create hero fantasies in order to go on living at all. The feelings of guilt were not to do with the fact that she had been a rebellious analysand, because she was definitely not that. Nor was she a hopeless case who had made extraordinary demands upon the strength of the analyst and had caused him to doubt his professional competence – not at all. Her guilt feelings took more the form, as she herself said, that she had driven him to his death because she had not realized her wish to pursue her education. She erected an entire structure of guilt feelings around this theme and explained to me in the greatest detail why this had driven the analyst to his death: he must have thought that she no longer had a way out. She spun another web of guilt around a potential relationship to a woman which she had not ventured to take up, even though the analyst encouraged her in this direction, or at least had not dissuaded her from it. In addition, she felt guilty because she had not lain in the sun as often as he had recommended and saw this as a factor contributing to his suicide. Naturally one can understand these guilt feelings in terms of an identification with the analyst. The analysand apparently perceived herself as a part of him and attempted to find out to what extent his suicide could have been her fault. But if one looks at these guilt feelings more closely, one sees that they pertain to decisions that she had not made or steps she had not taken as decisively as she might have wished. They pertain to things that really relate to her own life and that are certainly not irretrievably lost, as one who has died is. They are also things which, in reality, can hardly be seen as precipitating a suicide.

What is so clearly visible in the case of this analysand can also be seen in the guilt feelings of others who have been left behind. Guilt feelings can on the one hand genuinely refer back to things that were not realized in the relationship, so that one really is in fact culpable, but they can also relate to decisions and mistakes pertaining to one's own life.

Problems in the Phase of Search and Separation

The analysand Sylvia, whose analyst had committed suicide, went through an intensive phase of searching. She remarked, for example, that he had most certainly just been hidden by his wife, because she was jealous. She visited the widow once in order to determine whether she could discover something as to his whereabouts. She went to the grave to see if she could feel his presence there. She looked for him in his favorite café and where he went on vacation. This was conduct which she had never permitted herself while he was alive. Now that he was dead, she seemed driven by some force to search for him. She only found him in her dreams. There he was: polite, reserved, somewhat inhibited, and listening to her. In one dream she asked him how she could get him back. He waved to her and disappeared. Sylvia saw this dream as representing a challenge by the analyst to her to commit suicide. She developed an entire theory in support of the idea that this was the only way she could be with him.

While she worked out this theory and searched for him, without ever considering the aspect of separation, which was also contained in the dreams and to which I attempted to draw her attention, she developed a transference to me. When her theory was fully developed, she suddenly said during a therapy session, "The whole theory is useless; if I follow him, I lose you. And now I can't bear that either."

The danger of suicide seems to me to be greatest during the phase of searching. Even though very few individuals really commit suicide in the wake of a death, I believe nevertheless that the danger of "following" into death is actually very great in this phase. By "following" into death I mean that one offers no resistance to death. Parkes made an investigation in which he established that, in the first six months following the death of their wives, widowers die 40% more frequently than would be statistically expected.[54] This presumably suggests that in this situation life is found less attractive than death, which may in certain cases lead to suicide. Brown and Harris[55] have established that individuals who have lost a parent during early childhood tend later in life to react far more violently to the loss of a partner, and are perhaps more likely to commit suicide than those who are not so extremely influenced by an earlier loss. This stands to reason. Those who have already had to accept the loss of a parent or even a childhood friend at an early age, experienced while very young that life cannot be trusted, that everything is transient. When another loss occurs, these feelings rise to the surface again, and one is tempted then to find out if death is perhaps to be trusted more.

Sylvia at first developed a strong resentment towards me because I wasn't a man. She felt that, if I had been a man, she wouldn't have had to grieve so much for her former analyst: she could have simply "exchanged" him for me. She couldn't exchange him for me – and so she had to mourn. She attempted, however, to make this exchange again and again, and for this very reason, we recognized her relationship to the former analyst. Apparently he himself had been very depressive (Sylvia had sought him out because she suffered from depressive moods), and Sylvia over a period of time had become accustomed to asking him how he was feeling and to bringing him some offering to cheer him up.

I frustrated her enormously in that I explained to her that I didn't want to be cheered up by her; quite the contrary, I had planned to work with her on her problems. She found me rough and brutal. But she could see which strategies she had used with respect to her analyst, how much she had tried to play the strong one, and how far she, for this reason, was forced to cover up her weakness. She also saw that she had been overburdened by this. Outwardly she had asked for help, to be sure, but had then always attempted to place the analyst in the role of the one seeking help. Of course she employed this strategy not only in the analytical relationship. With this strategy she could always hide her own truths from herself but felt overburdened and consequently suffered from various psychosomatic complaints. She didn't permit herself to be taken care of, but she did permit her family to worry about her and take pity on her.

She became conscious not only of the strategy that she utilized, but also of how patient and indulgent her former analyst had been, how much it had fascinated her that someone could be so indulgent: he did not insist on helping, but let himself be helped instead. We agreed that this aspect of her former analyst could be something that she should try to discover in herself. Some dreams supported our idea, and she really tried to develop this aspect in her own life. It gave her a tremendous boost when she realized that this side of her really could play a part in her life – in a rudimentary way, of course, but it was still a visible beginning.

In Sylvia's case the phase of separation was delayed, because the transference to me took place. However it will come without fail, and it must be dealt with.

The danger in this phase seems to me really to be that the search will take place anyway. The person who has surrendered to the mourning process searches, without anyone having to tell him to do it. Perhaps he also finds – but the moment of separation will be difficult.

Precisely in therapeutic situations which are to help with mourning, it can happen that the process of mourning comes to a halt at the point where the mourner must separate from the deceased.

A thirty year old man, Philip, lost his mother. He had had a close relationship with her, and they had lived together. He was her only son. The mother was apparently very "motherly," and she had mothered him intensively until her death. Everyone expected a reaction of violent grief from him. But he displayed no grief whatsoever. In the beginning he travelled around the world and seemed to enjoy his freedom, emigrating later to take up a job in New Zealand. One day, without notifying anyone, he got on a plane to Europe and admitted himself to a psychiatric clinic because he could no longer handle his job. He said he had just left before they threw him out. He could no longer think, could no longer concen-

trate. Nothing gave him pleasure any more; he didn't know a soul in all the world – he had had enough. The clinic was also unsatisfactory; he had too little peace there. The psychiatrist advised him to come to me, and he did. He had, as it turned out, already lost his father when he was five years old. His sisters were at the time ten and twelve years old. The father had died at the age of sixty-seven, the mother being thirty-nine at the time. He could remember nothing of his father except that he had once received a ball from him, because he had behaved so well and had not disturbed the father while he was reading the newspaper. He described himself as a very quiet man, who never caused anyone any trouble. Everyone with whom he had worked held him in esteem. He was diligent enough, but not brilliant; he was suited for a middle management position, he knew that, and didn't wish for more. He had only a very superficial relationship to his sisters. They saw him as the little brother whom they could order around. He did not like to be ordered around; his mother had not ordered him around. Moreover, he had no memory of his mother. He had completely lost his memory when he climbed into the airplane. But that was all behind him now. Now he wanted to get to know a woman and marry. He wanted to live in his mother's house. His sisters had kept up the house while he was in New Zealand. Everything was just as it was before Mother's death, so he could live in his old room again. When I asked if he didn't want to rearrange the house, he replied that this was quite unnecessary, that he felt at home in the house, and he would only marry a woman who could also settle there.

It was clear to me that I had before me an individual who had not mourned. It was extraordinarily difficult to approach him. He felt nothing, he didn't want anything except a woman to marry. At first he presented no dreams, he had no fantasies. He also had no problems. He sat politely in his chair and waited to see what I had in mind for him.

I began to talk with him about his father. Aided by photos taken in early childhood, he began to remember a few of his father's characteristics. He became more and more animated as he talked about him. He began to ask friends of his parents and also his sisters about his father. He found out that his father must have been a rather mysterious individual, as everyone had a different impression of him. He began to write down the different views of his father and began to picture him in his imagination. He imagined taking trips with him and had arguments with him about political affairs. He found out, for instance, that his father had belonged to a political party that he particularly disliked. He could debate with his father for hours and regarded the views that his father expressed as genuine, completely real. Outwardly, a great change came over him: he became very active, began to participate in groups, rearranged his house, put some pieces of furniture that he didn't like so much in the basement. For me it was very difficult to find the right moment in which I could and would have to tell him that the father with whom he lived so intensely was actually his own inner figure; that the real father had died – and presumably had yet to be mourned. On the one hand, I found it good in a therapeutic sense that this young man, who had never had a relationship to his father and had apparently had no substitute father, was now able to identify with him and now seemed much more secure in his own identity. On the other hand, I felt this situation could not continue indefinitely. Separation would have to take place at some stage if he was really to find himself and deal with the problem he had with his mother. We hadn't spoken a single word about his mother.

A dream came to our aid. Philip, who rarely dreamt (or when he did, described these dreams in an extremely vague way), called me one morning, saying that he had to come to me right away – that he had had a horrible dream:

"I am with my father. I like my father tremendously and show this, by leaning on him and putting my arms around him tenderly. My father says: 'That's all right, son, but now you must let me go again.' "

Philip wept as he told the end of the dream and said that he felt as if his father had died that night. He also felt guilty, because the words of his father sounded as if he had burdened him, as if he should have altered his relationship to him long ago.

I explained to him that the separation had certainly not taken place before time and that now he would almost certainly go through the phases of mourning that I had described to him. He was relieved that I apparently knew what was going to happen to him. But then he didn't keep so strictly to my schematic representation of the process of mourning. The phase of denial didn't occur, and the phase of emotional chaos, combined with searching lasted a long time. This required submersion again in the fantasy relationship with his father, then leaving this behind once more, because he felt that this type of relationship wasn't possible for him any more. I attempted to show him that this father with whom he had made long fantasy journeys, with whom he had debated, remained part of his own personality. Nine months after this dream, he began to realize this and thus became calmer. He could only really believe it when a friend of his parents told him that he was becoming more and more like his father. With this, he began to see himself more intensely in terms of similarities to his father, but also sought to discover those traits which distinguished and separated him from his father. Strong identification with the father occurred repeatedly. For instance, he knew that his father had married for the first time at thirty-five. Philip was now convinced that he would also marry for the first time at thirty-five. He took it for granted that, like his father, he would also marry twice.

Even at this stage we see the difficulty in his ability to separate himself from the dead father, a separation which should involve the idea that the father's life is not simply taken over as a blueprint for oneself. The biggest difficulty would arise when we began to deal with the image of the dead mother in exactly the same way. He had struck the mother right out of his life: "That's over and done with now." With this, he had disposed of her loss. It had become clear to him in the meantime that his trip to New Zealand had something to do with the death of the mother and that his psychic breakdown also was the result of his avoiding the grief connected with her death.

At first Philip made great progress in remembering his mother. More and more came back to him in connection with her. He began to see the way she had ordered him about, though in a much more subtle way than the sisters had done. Above all, of course, she had done it with much more love, and had demanded much more love in return. He fantasized extensively about his mother, reproaching her, but also declaring solemnly that he would never leave her, that he would marry a woman who was just like her. Philip found photographs of his mother as a young woman and began to look around for girls who were similar to her. These young ladies, however, wanted nothing to do with him. I said to him that this might be because he couldn't approach these young women armed with these pre-conditions. He would be better off asking himself quite spontaneously whether he liked a woman or not. As relationships were established, Philip always ascertained after approximately four weeks, "Again, she isn't what my mother would have wanted." And, "When I have spent an evening with my mother in my imagination, I feel better than when I have spent an evening with a girl; sex is neither here nor there." It was clear to me that Philip wanted to go on living with his mother, that he wanted to continue as a unit with her, and that his attempt to find a girl who was similar to his mother could never lead to a relationship. Through the col-

95

lapse of these relationships he could remain symbiotic with the mother.

I told him a fairy-tale which I felt showed that persevering in a relationship with someone who is deceased can pull one out of life.

The Beloved Spouse [55a]

Once upon a time there was a man and a woman who lived in peace and harmony with one another and liked each other so much that life could not have been any better. As life continued, they spoke together, and the man said to the woman, "If I die, you will take another man as husband." And the wife replied, "And you will certainly take another wife; you won't remain unwed." But neither believed the other, and they made an agreement that neither would marry again. Then the wife died. At first the man lived without a woman, because he truly felt he didn't want to marry again. But as time went by he thought, "Why should I mourn for her? I will marry again." And he found another woman. As he was about to celebrate the wedding, it struck him, "Oh, I do want to go to my wife to bid her farewell and to ask the dead for forgiveness." The bride was left standing at the church while the man visited his dead wife. He went and knelt by the grave: "Forgive me! I am going to my wedding ceremony. I am marrying again." The grave opened, and the wife called him to her, "Come, come! Don't be afraid, come here!" She called him into the grave and said to him, "Don't you remember that we promised that the one who remained behind would never again marry?" And she bade him sit upon the coffin. Then the woman in the grave asked him, "Would you like some wine?" She gave him a cup, and the man drank. When he wanted to take leave of her, she pleaded, "Stay a while, and let us have a cozy chat." She filled his cup a second

96

time, and the man drank again. He stood up again and wanted to leave, but again she said, "Let us chat a while longer!" And the man stayed and chatted. At home the others held a service because they believed the man had died. The bride waited and waited and finally went back to her parents. The dead wife filled his cup a third time and again bade him tarry. Finally she let him go: "Go on, then!" And the man went away. He went to the church, but the minister was no longer there; there was no one at all, and he himself was as gray as an old hoopoe bird, because he had been in the grave for thirty years.

Philip was very thoughtful after I told him this fairy-tale. He asked sadly, "I suppose you mean that I have gray hair, too?" Then it suddenly struck him that he could recall nothing at all of the funeral; thus it was absurd to think that he was sitting in the grave with his mother. He had never even been to her grave. He wasn't even sure whether his sisters hadn't simply hidden the mother. He took offense at my telling him this fairy-tale, but began a very intensive effort to come to grips with what had in fact happened at the funeral. With one of his sisters he once visited the mother's grave, but he found nothing there at all – his mother was definitely not there.

Then came vacation. I had been preparing Philip for weeks for the fact that I would go on vacation. In view of his separation problems, I expected that the interruption of therapy would be very unpleasant for him. Philip reacted very understandingly at first; we discussed how he could reach me at any time, whereupon he stressed that he would, of course, only do that in an emergency.

In the last week before the vacation he came to the session very sullen and prone to tears, and suddenly said, "I forbid you to go on vacation! If you want to go anyway, you must find me a therapist who is exactly like you." It struck me that he had wanted a wife who would be just like his mother, and that he had now evidently transferred the mother to me. Now he wanted to remain symbiotic with me; I was not permitted to leave him, this separation couldn't take place, unless I offered him an alternative symbiosis of "equal value." It was now clear to me that he had in fact resented his mother for not providing him with a substitute of "equal value." She had died without making it possible for him to enter into a symbiotic relationship with a woman who would be of equal value to him. He had expected something from his mother, and he still expected that the dead mother should be able to fulfill his wish. On the other hand, he expected me as therapist to behave as his mother should have behaved. I was not allowed to go away, and presumably I was also not expected to find him a wife.

We discussed his forbidding me to go on vacation, which seemed absurd even to him. Philip himself realized that he did not want to separate from me: during his life he had had to separate from people too often. He immediately added that, if he were ever able to find himself a wife, then they would not be separated from one another even for one second. I attempted to explain this fear of abandonment to him as the fear that I also could simply go away, die, and then he would again be alone. I should prepare for this eventuality and find for him a suitable replacement. I tried to explain to him that his symbiotic longings for his mother had been displaced and transferred to me. He replied sarcastically, "Well, at least we are sitting together in your practice instead of in the grave; that, at least, is progress." I rejoined that I was not the woman in the grave, and needed to have my vacation. He breathed a sigh of relief and said that he would have felt really guilty if I had stayed behind on his account. This showed me that his symbiotic needs were linked to a great deal of guilt. He himself seemed to sense that these needs stood in the way of his life.

After the vacation he told me he had discovered that he could actually cope very well with being separated from me; the situation as it was described in the fairy-tale was now ended, and he was thinking about ending therapy. I asked him if he could see a connection between his departure for New Zealand after the death of the mother and his wish to break off therapy at this point. To this he replied that he saw the parallel, of course, but it was not quite the same: if it had been he would have had to take off for New Zealand or break off therapy immediately after my departure. But he hadn't done this; instead he had given a great deal of thought to the fairy-tale, and he had been really angry the whole time, because there had been no progress in the matter of finding a wife. Thus, he had not conducted himself exactly as before, but somewhat better. I was happy to admit this and mentioned that aggression with respect to me was also something new; he had scarcely permitted himself aggression towards his mother. His wish to end therapy was also an act of aggression. In any case he had to ask himself if "New Sea-land," which in our work together had become a symbol for a new beginning, for a country wrung from the unconscious, new ground that one could tread and make fruitful, was really attainable this time. I myself felt a great resistance to breaking off therapy at this point, all the more because it seemed clear to me that his impulse to break off therapy was the reaction, "Before you abandon me again, I am going to abandon you." I told him this, and also let him know that it would hurt me a great deal if he now broke off therapy, because I particularly wanted to solve the problem of symbiosis with him. I added that I could in no way force him to continue.

This communication of mine visibly relieved him. He relaxed, leaned back in his chair and said he would think it over again. If I only had suggested a solution to his problem of finding a wife, then he presumably would not have needed any time to think it over.

At this point I introduced the idea that he must have blamed his mother for not having found a wife for him and that now he was angry at me for the same reason: because I had not provided him with a wife. This remark made him think. He admitted that in the airplane he had repeated a peculiar sentence to himself: "When you have found me a wife, then I will come back." He wondered if this could have to do with an unconscious expectation that his mother find a wife for him. He felt even now that she could give him some sort of sign from the Hereafter. As for me, he didn't hold out much hope that I would, because I always stressed how essential it was that he make his own decisions.

In the sessions which followed he didn't mention wanting to break off therapy again. On the one hand he accused me of having abandoned him, while on the other, he showed interest in the fairy-tale about the "beloved spouse." It tormented him that the fairy-tale indicated no way of saving the situation. I tried to point out to him that this symbiosis had come about because from the very beginning both the marriage partners had wanted to avoid any change and were not ready to accept death as the ultimate change in life. He responded dryly: "That was the way it was with me once." We now discussed the fact that, in the relationship described in the fairy-tale, aggression was completely excluded, although it expressed itself in death fantasies. We emphasized the importance of aggression as a means of achieving distance, of delimiting oneself and making known one's requirements. Philip breathed a sigh of relief. He had in the meantime developed a few aggressive feelings of his own.

The fairy-tale describes the beginning of a mourning process: the bereaved mourns and turns his attention in the end to a new woman. But then the man is overwhelmed by his memories, feels guilty because he has changed, and because he could not keep the promise which he had once given. A relapse occurs, a regression into the grave. The dead cannot be dead, the living cannot live, bygones cannot be bygones. Aggression in the sense of decisive action is missing here as well, and so the "loyal" husband sits for years in the grave. Instead of taking leave, really saying farewell, instead of accepting the guilt over the fact that he has changed and now thinks differently, he destroys his own life.

Philip talked about the fact that, in going to New Zealand, he had actually wanted to make this separation complete. But he had gone about it in the wrong way, and only outwardly had made the separation, which he should also have made inwardly. Clearly he had not been capable of this at that point in time because the relationship was so intense. Because of the early death of his father and the unaccomplished mourning for him, neither identification with, nor separation from him had been possible. The result was that he remained dependent in "taking care" of the mother.

There followed a phase in which Philip was very sad. He had become very conscious of the fact that his mother really had died, that she was no longer there, and thus could no longer help him find a wife. It was also clear to him that a woman just like his mother was not to be found. In separation experiences with me he learned that parting did not mean that the other person died. Slowly he developed faith in a certain continuity in life and in relationships. He often dreamed now of a motherly woman, whom he definitely did not associate with this mother. One of these dreams is representative of others which followed.

"I am sitting on a stone and thinking hard about something. Each time, just as I think I have the result, I forget again what I am thinking about. Then an old woman comes along, older than my mother and with an old-fashioned hairstyle. She gives me bread to eat, and I just can't understand why I have to think so strenuously."

He has to think so hard because, in the meantime, he has found a young woman and has entered into a casual relationship with her. This relationship activates the entire symbiosis problem with his mother again. After at first experiencing feelings of guilt because, through this rela-

101

tionship, he is "untrue" to the mother and to me, these guilt feelings were then alleviated by another dream, in which the mother and the father congratulated him on his choice of young lady. He now entered into a very symbiotic relationship with the young woman herself. This showed itself in that he forbade his friend to go away alone for a few days, as he was extraordinarily jealous. If they ever had differences of opinion, he became immediately uncertain and brooded all day long as to whether this were the right woman for him or not.

The dream seems to provide an answer to this question, in that it suggests that he should think less and accept instead solid nourishment: bread. I see in the old motherly woman his own potential to be nurturing and motherly with respect to his own needs, instead of tormenting himself with brooding. The dreamer associated "eating bread" with the fact that his mother from time to time referred to certain things as being "as easy as eating bread." This statement and the emotional content of the dream convinced Philip that he had worried far too much, and that he really should have a bit more faith. I tried to explain to him that, because of his past history, he would always have the tendency to cling symbiotically to his partner. He would continue to expect everything from this partner, and must always be prepared to "separate" from the partner, when the time for a separation came.

After Philip married and had received a job offer in another city, we decided to terminate therapy. We gave ourselves three months time for this final phase, because it could be foreseen that for a person with this type of "abandonment complex" a separation would not be accomplished without difficulty. That had been shown in the separation before the vacation, and to a lesser extent, also in the separation difficulties at the end of each session. Philip would attempt to postpone the end of the hour by bringing up any sort of highly important problem.

Philip was at first very sad and lamented that it was

always the same in life: one entered into relationships only to part again; actually, he would have been better off if he had killed himself in New Zealand. But then he laughed and remarked that it really was strange because now he had far more joy in life and even had a wife. In the next breath he complained that at the time I had refused to help him in any way to find a wife, in the way he had imagined it. He had also suffered a great deal because he could not simply live with me for the duration of therapy. That had been his wish: to live with me, to have gone on vacation with me. We discussed once again in this context the time when he had transferred the relationship with his dead mother to me, and how difficult that had been for him, but also how important. He expressed his disappointment about the fact that I was never ready simply to "rescue" him like a son in any situation. He spoke about times when I had made him angry because I had treated him as one would a child; but at the same time he complained about the fact that at other times I had demanded too much of him. All the time he was considering whether he had projected the mother onto me, or whether I had in fact really let him down. I did not fail to mention the way I myself had experienced this situation, and also discussed with him where I felt I really had made mistakes. He could now cope well with the idea that I had made mistakes: yes, he even seemed to be rather glad about it. He learned to see me as a real person, with my potential and my limitations. He mentioned in passing that he could now put up with his wife's weaknesses much better.

We went through the phases of therapy again together, mentioning the phase of mourning for his lost father only peripherally. We discussed at this point what therapy had accomplished and what it had not accomplished: Philip still tended to form symbiotic relationships, even to his superiors, and to demand too much from these superiors as a result. Philip had expected that by the end of therapy he would be the sort of man "whom nothing fazes." By the end of therapy he could deal well with his symbiotic

103

requirements and with his abandonment fears and separation problems, but naturally he remained very sensitive in this respect, reacting to "separation" when no one else would have even perceived the situation as a separation. For example, a birthday was a very difficult day for him, because he had to take leave of the "old" year of his life. When he noticed a creeping sadness, it now occurred to him that a separation situation was approaching; he mourned consciously, became furious about transiency, and afterwards felt in a better mood.

An essential result of therapy for Philip was that he felt he could separate from me with the certainty that he would not really lose me, as the therapy had become an integral part of his life. He had integrated the way we had approached and questioned his problems during therapy. Still more important to him was that through his dreams, and they were very impressive dreams, it was made clear that he did not have to take every decision alone. For this reason, when faced with too much responsibility or when too many demands were made of him, he no longer needed to take refuge in some form of symbiotic relationship. In his dreams he experienced new aspects of himself. These became very important to him, signifying and bringing about a tremendous opening-up. He now felt that his own inner self supported him much better than his mother had ever been able to support him, and better also than I as therapist had been able to.

This phase of reflecting on his therapy and our parting was accompanied throughout by feelings of mourning, both on his part and mine. I had the feeling of having travelled a long road with Philip. I had learned a great deal from him about mourning, about the paralyzing feeling that oppresses an individual who cannot mourn. Because of Philip I was repeatedly forced to confront symbiosis and to find ways which would lead out of symbiosis. To end therapy was a sacrifice for me, too, but one that had to be made, because the process was concluded.

Bringing therapy to a close was, for Philip, bound up with the experience of death to a far greater extent than I had experienced with other analysands. It was a test of his ability to let a person go who had meant something to him and not lose himself in the process. It would show whether he could become more aware of himself in the process in spite of a repeated necessity to part, and would commit himself to a life of involvement with others. In the final analysis, it would show whether he wants to *live,* even if death plays an important role in that life. Venturing into a new relationship is the test of whether the mourning process has succeeded.

I have described the concluding phase of this therapy in more detail, because it seems to me that the conclusion of therapy concerns leave-taking in a wider context – death in the broadest sense. This phase, especially with individuals who have problems with leave-taking and with mourning, must be handled carefully if the conclusion of therapy is not to be experienced as yet another situation in which one simply loses someone and oneself at the same time.

SYMBIOSIS AND INDIVIDUATION

That the mourner either hopes to find the deceased, or in one way or another tries to fuse with him, is a part of every mourning process. In this way life, which had become intolerable because of the loss, can go on. By choosing death oneself or fantasizing about it, one can also bring about a union with the one whom one has lost. In any case it is a matter of fusion with the deceased, an attempt to undo the loss and go on living as if nothing has happened.

In Philip's case, these symbiotic tendencies were especially visible, at first with respect to his mother, later in the transference to me. Volkan,[56] in his description of his short-term therapy method with individuals who have not mourned and are thus showing depressive, psychosomatic or psychotic reactions, stresses that it must be clearly distinguished in an early phase of therapy what belongs to the deceased and what belongs to the mourner. An attempt must be made to dissolve the fusion and define the individual with respect to the deceased.

By "symbiosis" I mean the fusion of an individual with another individual, or the fusion of a group with a particular idea, country, dead person, etc. This fusion can go so far that everything which distinguishes and separates appears to be obliterated. The two entities indulge one another and permit nothing to intrude which could spoil this togetherness. This union with another, this attempt at primal security, is a fake which must be continuously maintained, usually at the cost of total accommodation. In the specific case of the symbiosis of a mourner with his deceased partner, this means that nothing may change with the death of the partner. It can even mean that the mourner can at last let a relationship unfold in complete symbiosis, which was impossible as long as the partner was alive and made his own demands upon the relationship.

According to my observations it is not only those mourners who during their lifetimes had a symbiotic relationship to their partners who tend to this fusion with the deceased. There seems to be a stage of longing for symbiotic fusion that almost every mourner must go through at first.

Naturally one must ask in this connection to what extent the mourner, given that his life and self-perception have been disrupted, needs to experience himself as "whole." We tend anyway to project the human longing for "oneness," be it with oneself, with the Divine, or with the cosmos, onto the partner. During this time of upheaval this longing is even more likely to be projected directly onto the deceased partner. A great deal is thereby achieved – supposedly. The deceased remains, the experience of "oneness" between oneself and the partner is temporarily maintained, life need not be altered. But because of this, the mourning process comes to a halt, and this in turn leads to various psychological problems, depression in particular.[57]

By comparing this with the phase of "normal symbiosis" in the life of an individual, it must be possible to get an indication of how such a long-lasting entanglement with the deceased could be dissolved. Mahler repeatedly describes the phase of "normal" symbiosis of the infant, from approximately the second month on, in which the infant behaves as if he and the mother comprise "one omnipotent system – a duality within a shared boundary."[58] The phase of symbiosis is followed by the phase of separation, within which a convergence again takes place. What Mahler describes in the infant seems to me to apply to a generally valid natural rhythm: phases of separation and individuation are always followed by phases of increased striving for symbiosis. Separation, according to Mahler, Pine and Bergman,[59] means emerging from the state of fusion, and individuation means the achievement of individual characteristics. Within the separation phase, a phase of convergence often reoccurs, as if one has to assure oneself that there is still a way back. In the new phase of development, reached by acquiring individual attributes, the need for symbiosis exists once again. This should be lived out as the optimal symbiosis, as a precondition for a renewed separation and individuation – and not only during the stage of infancy.

Symbiotic tendencies in our everyday life take so many forms and occur so frequently that we cannot simply view symbiosis as pathological. We can assume that symbiosis, on the one hand, and development out of the symbiosis in the direction of individuation, on the other, really correspond to a life rhythm. For this reason it seems important to me not simply to avoid symbiosis, but rather to attempt to live it to the full. Even with the small child an optimal symbiosis is the precondition for an optimal separation and individuation.

The question can now be asked as to whether the mourner who desires symbiosis with the departed is the sort of individual who, in his life, never succeeded in living out a form of optimal symbiosis, or whether his need for symbiosis is the result of the tremendous shock he has suffered. It seems that the constant acquisition of new characteristics can make the individual independent, and also lonely, and that this very individuation in turn awakens in him a longing for symbiosis. With this in mind, it seems that losing a loved one forces a step in the direction of individuation, and thus awakens a longing for symbiosis. Because it is not a joyful step, taken on one's own initiative, it must be expected that a step backwards will at first be made.

It is interesting in this connection that our collective conceptions regarding the Hereafter lie very close to our conceptions regarding symbiosis. Paradise, for example, in that everyone lives together in peace, is doubtless an image that also lies behind our longing for symbiosis. We use, for example, expressions like: "entering into eternal bliss," "becoming part of a greater glory," where we are then to be "comforted and sustained." This longing for peace underlies the collective conception of the Hereafter as does the striving for symbiosis. It is a longing to be cared for, a longing to be sheltered, for fusion with something greater which gathers us to it. Even in the existential view, according to which the human being upon his death becomes "a thing among things," this factor seems to be present.[60]

We can apparently only tolerate the thought of death if we can simultaneously imagine that death lets us merge with something greater than ourselves. So it is small wonder that we also long for symbiosis, when we experience death as mourners.

Nevertheless, differences among mourners can be observed. We should bear in mind that the mourner who understands mourning as a process can move out of the phase of symbiosis in the direction of a new individuation, and that in this way he also becomes capable of relationship again. But another hardens in the condition of symbiosis and feels increasingly sad and devoid of meaning, as a symbiotic connection can only offer protection and strength at a certain time and for a limited amount of time.

In order to look at this situation more closely it seems necessary to me to explain what is meant by the concept, "optimal symbiosis." A symbiosis is "optimal" when an individual can have an experience of fusion, out of which he emerges strengthened, so that he can again confront the changing demands of life with new potential for relationship and new self-awareness.

We find, for example, an optimal form of symbiosis among mystics. The mystical experience is a fusion of the mystic with the Divine, total absorption in a greater wholeness. This longing of the mystic has often been described as a longing for death: the mystic longs for death in order to be with his God. Nevertheless, this did not hinder many mystics (despite, or perhaps because of, their relationship to

110

God) from being autonomous personalities in the psychological sense. They worked fearlessly among their fellows, fearless presumably because they had had precisely this experience of fusion which imparts the feeling of security, significance and clarity. St. Paul wrote in a letter to the Philippians,[61] " ... I am torn between the desire to depart and be with Christ, which would be by far the best thing, and the need to remain in the flesh for your sake."

Teresa of Avila is a further example. She describes a mystical experience:[62]

"As I was once just at the point of reciting the hymn, 'Veni Creator Spiritus,' I was overcome by an ecstasy of such violence that it almost robbed me of my senses, an experience that I can in no way doubt, because it was far too public. At the same time, I heard the words, 'I do not want you to keep company with humans any more but only with angels.' This filled me with terror."

This mystical experience seems to me to be a fusion experience combined with the temptation to remain in the symbiosis. ("I do not want you to keep company with humans...") The terror appears to lead Teresa back into the world. It no doubt pointed out to her the difference between her experience of mystical fusion and her task as she perceived it in this world, and which she pursued with tremendous energy and purpose. We cannot accuse Teresa of being only symbiotic and not individuated.

Perhaps the mystics have experienced symbiosis in a way which enhances life and really removes the smallness and fragility of the human being. However, it is not possible to linger too long in such a symbiosis, for religious experiences and the experience of God, by reason of their nature, elude any hold, remain unattainable, thus pose no threat to separation and individuation. Still, the mystic, in accordance with his vision, wants to illuminate this world for his God, and change it.

Optimal symbiosis could thus be experienced where an individual succeeds in transforming the longing of the small child for the mother into a longing for transcendence and into the opportunity to fuse with this transcendent. Whatever name he gives this transcendent, he draws strength from it, so as to be able to conduct himself as autonomously as possible in his everyday world. The need for fantasies of greatness and grandiosity, which is stressed so heavily in the discussion of narcissism,[63] is understandable as a need for a symbiotic fusion with the transcendent, which would lend the individual a "natural" greatness, which he needs in view of his mortality. In this fusion with the transcendent the individual must not prove his grandiosity and suffer because he does not fulfill its demands; he shares in a greatness, from which he nevertheless differentiates himself.

An optimal symbiosis can also be experienced in eroticism and sexuality. It is a matter of fusion with another individual, of a dissolution of the borders of the ego, of a merging with a greater wholeness. Meyer[64] sees in the mystical and in the erotic experience, as well as in the experience of alienation, anticipatory fantasies about death. Criteria for this are the loss of ego boundaries, destabilization of the ego identity and the standing still of time. These events are sometimes experienced with fear, sometimes more in fascination as an expansion of the personality.[65] Meyer agrees with Georges Bataille[66] when he states that, because of the realities of death and individuality, a discontinuous element occurs in the life of the individual, whereby, in the face of mortality, a longing for continuity develops. It is this continuity which is achieved in the erotic and in the mystical experience. In these experiences the formation and dissolution of boundaries exist in a rhythmic alternation with one another. Meyer brings death into relation with this experience of the continuity, the Oneness, which I call optimal symbiosis, and thereby refers to the great theme of world literature: love and death.[67] At the moment of the deepest experience of wholeness and the most profound feeling of being alive, the presence of death will also be felt, for there would not be an experience of totality, if life and death were not experienced together. Rilke expresses this in his poem, "Conclusion"[68] :

> *"Death is great.*
> *We are his*
> *when we are laughing.*
> *When we feel ourselves to be*
> *in the midst of life,*
> *he dares to weep*
> *within us."*

According to Meyer, similar extreme events, comparable to erotic or mystical fusion experiences, can appear quite spontaneously – in a dream, for example.[69] On this subject Jung would have spoken of an experience of the "Self."[70] By "Self" Jung understood the unity and wholeness of the personality that transcends consciousness and which, in special moments – be they in dreams or in everyday occurrences – can be experienced as the dissolving of the ego boundary. This is experienced as a feeling of wholeness, also as a suspension of time, so that in this moment the entire past and the entire future are present and are experienced as timeless. This experience of totality grips, sustains and gives meaning. "Awakening" from this experience does not annul it, but the loneliness of the ego, the ego's being thrown back upon itself, will now be experienced painfully. Mourning for the condition of wholeness sets in as a longing for the experience of fullness which has vanished. Bound up with this is a longing for death as a possible way of regaining the lost wholeness. It is a fundamental point of Jungian psychology that a tension exists between the experience of the Self, a wholeness, or fusion with something transcendental, which gives meaning, and the experience of the ego, which is mortal and has little continuity. The ego,

113

which must exist in a relationship with this Self, must not let fascination with the Self paralyze it. The ego must not, for example, simply surrender to the longing for death, but can and must realize itself in life. It was for this reason, it seems to me, that Jung did not postulate a death drive, as Freud did. One could say that, in this conception of the Self, the greatest possible enhancement of libido, the greatest possible impulse toward life, exists in union with the experience of death.

The works of Grof and Halifax are interesting in this respect. They did therapeutic work with individuals suffering from incurable cancer, researching the effects of LSD. They found with these patients that dramatic changes in the conception of death and the attitude toward death resulted. Under the influence of the drug, "they experienced the death of the ego; they experienced rebirth and the cosmic unity."[71] Death lost some of its terror; the possibility of a continuation beyond death became imaginable. They "developed a strong belief in the unity of the creation."[72]

These "cosmic visions" can be seen in relation to the experience of the "Self," as described repeatedly by Jung.[73] Symbiosis with the Self would thus have a healing and meaningful effect. We easily find the way out of this symbiosis; we fall out of it involuntarily, as out of the religious experience. Precisely because of this, the longing for this symbiosis can be dangerous. I see in addiction to drugs just such a longing for the state of symbiosis with the Self.

But symbiosis will not only be experienced where I regard it as optimal, that is, where the rhythm of symbiosis, separation and further development is ensured. We are more likely to transfer our longing for symbiosis onto every sort of relationship. I don't regard this as wrong. It is only problematic when it is not succeeded by separation. This can happen when one feels that life has not been enhanced to a significant degree. Perhaps a wholeness is sought that cannot be fulfilled in symbiosis with another individual.

Finding the way out of symbiosis is also difficult for

those individuals who have never been granted a symbiosis. A child who did not experience fusion with the mother will have difficulty in developing autonomy, as will a child whose mother will not release it from symbiosis.[74] Such experiences will have an influence on the way separation is experienced and on the achievement of autonomy later in life. Because this striving for symbiosis, as well as for separation and individuation, is a perpetual rhythm of psychic development in humans, steps toward individuation will always be endangered when too little symbiosis is granted. This can also mean that it is sought in the wrong place. It could be that we are too exclusive in wanting to have our symbiotic requirements met by a human being and thus project the need for fusion with something transcendent onto the partner. Certainly it is true that, through the experience of love, a fusion with something transcendent can be experienced, but it is not the partner himself who must fulfill this longing. It is in the relationship to the partner that this experience of the transcendent can come to pass. But if we view the partner as the one who must fulfill our symbiotic needs, then we demand from him a magnitude and something absolute which overburdens him.[75] The rhythm of symbiosis, separation and individuation is then disturbed, because the times of separation and distancing from the partner, the times in which one could discover new potentials, are only experienced as deficits. It is precisely these times that can provide the precondition to experiencing the transcendent in a new form in the old partner.

Thus it can be that, if satisfaction of the symbiotic requirement is expected in the wrong place, the phases of separation and individuation are reached only with difficulty. This of course poses the question as to whether those individuals who can permit an optimal symbiosis are also the individuals for whom the process of mourning proceeds undisturbed. To my knowledge there have been as yet no investigations into this question.

A further reason for lingering in symbiosis with the dead

partner is fear of the future. If mourning really means a massive change in the way one perceives life and oneself, and there is no doubt about this, and if, in addition, we consider how chaotic the emotions accompanying mourning are, then it is not surprising that a retreat into symbiosis occurs in the beginning. Behind it lies the right impulse. If we perceive symbiosis with something transcendent as a feeling of wholeness, as providing a feeling of support and the greatest enhancement of life, then it is appropriate to seek out this condition in order afterwards to be able to cope with the process of mourning more easily. By means of the symbiotic fusion, the mourner reassures himself that he is safe, that he is "sustained," and being ultimately sustained, can increase his potential with respect to life. He has been swept into the whirlpool of grief, must accomplish a separation, take his leave and separate himself from the many familiar habits that he has come to love. But even in this situation the symbiosis can be sought in the wrong place; that is, with the deceased, with the life that is now past. It is as if, in searching for an object with which we can symbiotically fuse, our reach is always too short, and thus we naturally remain unsatisfied.

A further problem that can result in an individual's remaining "stalled" in the symbiotic relationship with the deceased is caused by the fact that he has already suffered separation too often. As a reason why he didn't want to let me go on vacation, Philip stated that he had already had to separate too often in life. As mentioned earlier, Brown and Harris[76] indicated that those individuals who had lost someone very near to them during their childhood reacted far more sensitively than others to subsequent losses and separations. They also developed neurotic symptoms more frequently, particularly depression. Symbiotic lingering with the deceased has the effect that new relationships neither can nor may be entered into. In this way one is protected from further separations. One deals with the fear of loss by anxiously clinging to what is already lost. But in so

116

doing, one dries up emotionally; life becomes empty and meaningless. Is there a way out of these symbiotic relationships which no longer offer any incentive to live, are merely a prison and don't permit any further development? Because the symbiotic relationship to the deceased has become a prison, both inwardly and outwardly, a social isolation often sets in. The outside world does not accept this symbiotic relationship, thus these individuals who cannot integrate their grief seek help. The rooms that have not been changed since the death of the loved one are a symbol for the standstill in the life of the mourner. In my opinion, the expulsion from the symbiosis takes place in this situation, as in all symbiotic relationships, precisely because the symbiosis has become exaggerated. In order for one to be able to remain symbiotic with the deceased, the deceased must generally be highly idealized. Aggressions are therefore not experienced, the mourner becomes depressive and seeks help. Seeking help admits another individual to the symbiotic system. In these cases it is generally the help of a therapist, and therapy can of course be approached in many ways. Volkan, a specialist in the area of belated mourning, deals with delayed mourning in short-term therapy (about 32 hours in the course of two months). He stresses that in an early phase of therapy a distinction must be made between the deceased and the self. Thus he himself introduces aggression into the process in that he demands this radical separation.

In Philip's case the symbiotic situation with his mother was transferred to me. Because I didn't behave the way he expected me to as "substitute mother," a great deal of aggression was experienced. He was also confronted with aspects which had not played a part in the symbiotic situation, because of the simple fact that I was a different individual than his mother had been, with different expectations and values. It was certainly important for Philip in the beginning to feel strengthened in his masculinity through identification with his father. The way out of the symbiosis

117

was for him a long and difficult path as, due to the excessively strong bond with his mother, he had a tendency to symbiotic lingering to start with. The early death of his father probably reinforced this tendency, combined presumably with the mother's wish to keep this son by her side to replace the father, thus curtailing his striving for autonomy.

In some cases it struck me that a brief symbiotic phase with the deceased partner set in during the phase of searching-finding-separating. The deceased became an inner partner for discussion who, however, changed more and more over a period of time and became an inner "guide figure" with whom the mourner could again be symbiotic. This especially impressed me in the therapy of a forty-two year old woman who was very attached to her father. She had looked after him until his death and had never entered into a relationship with anyone else. She was referred to me by a doctor because of "heart troubles" for which no physical cause could be found. She lived in the conviction that her father would care for her from the "Hereafter," that her life could go on as before, and that mourning as experienced by other individuals was in fact ridiculous. Such people simply didn't have the imagination necessary to carry on a relationship beyond death. Her father appeared in her dreams, and more and more frequently was accompanied by a young woman who, although she resembled the dreamer, also represented a sort of "alter ego," who behaved in ways the dreamer would never have behaved. This dream woman engaged in lively discussions with the father, danced ecstatically, flirted with men – in short, did all those things which the dreamer, in remembrance of her father and out of love for him, had never done. This dream figure radiated strength and became a figure of great importance for the dreamer. This dream woman led her into those areas of life that previously had been neglected because of the symbiotic relationship to the father. Out of the daughter was born the woman; the symbiotic relationship to the father dissolved.

118

The dreamer felt then that she had really lost the father, but in exchange had gained immeasurably in life.

These inner guide figures tend to be of the same sex as the dreamer and often embody that part of life which was avoided in the symbiotic situation. For this reason they cause fear, but are at the same time invigorating. Those aspects of life that were not permitted manifest themselves at first as convincing images in dreams and then spill over into real life. Behind these figures a tremendous strength is hidden. These inner guide figures remind one of the magical helpers in fairy-tales,[77] of brother figures like Gilgamesh and Enkidu.[78] These magical helpers are at first presented in the fairy-tales as individuals who have died but have not been buried as they still owe a debt to the living in some way. They become helpful figures as soon as someone releases them, as soon as someone sees to it that the dead really may be dead, as soon as the redemption takes place. By way of thanks they involve the hero in life, making possible a tremendous growth in his personality – and are then needed no longer. They represent aspects of the hero that had been left out of his life, and they apparently also know what fate intends for this hero. They represent a force which transcends the human and are experienced as providence.

These figures can also be experienced in dreams, and they have the ability to involve the dreamer in precisely those aspects of life which he has avoided until now. They generally bring a new way of behaving, a readiness to take risks, a healthy aggression, joy in living and pleasure in one's body, and thus an increased self-awareness which means that one must no longer constantly seek a way back into symbiosis. The redeemed dead person becomes, in the fairy-tale, the "grateful dead," a helpful companion both in dreams and in everyday life.

Often the person of the analyst is woven into this inner companion figure. In these cases it seems to me to be important that the final phase of therapy be perceived and

119

conducted with special care. The separation from the therapist should have a strengthening effect, so the patient can
rejoice in the fact that so much autonomy has been
achieved, that life can once again be dealt with without help.
But it is also important that the dreamer recognize in these
dream figures a form that, for a specific period of time, has
the task of involving him in life and developing him in this
way; that this figure is a psychic reality which cannot simply be "used," that it will disappear again, and that here too
a separation will be necessary. It is true that such inner
guide figures appear when we need them. But we may not
require them always to appear in the same form, as the
individual who has a strong need for symbiosis typically
does. He also wants to fuse symbiotically with these
figures, which is certainly appropriate for a certain period of
time and can enhance life. But if the individual permits no
change, the inner companion figure who was at first so full
of life and strength will become a lifeless image which,
nevertheless, continues to impose its rules and restrictions
on life. Here, too, it is important to maintain the rhythm of
symbiosis, separation and individuation.

It is certainly not the case that only mourners are in
danger of "stalling" in symbiosis, of holding on to what is
past, to what can no longer and must no longer be changed.
Symbiosis is always sought as protection against change in
life. Fear of continual change, fear of the need for continual
leave-taking and the continual "need to die," causes us to
seek out something permanent, which we then want to be
more than something that simply remains. This fear causes
us to seek out the symbiotic relationship that is meant to
"rescue" us from the natural rhythm of life.

The tendency of the mourner to withdraw into a symbiotic relationship with the deceased seems to me to demonstrate existentially most clearly that we oppose the radical
demand for change. We do this by lingering too long in a
symbiotic situation, a symbiosis which we often want to
create with an unsuitable "host." Thus, it is absolutely nec-

essary that we find that optimal symbiosis which really permits a development of our personality, which brings with it an increased joy in living and which does not operate as a restriction, in the way that many symbiotic situations do, because of forced adaptation to the partner.

MAKING A COMMITMENT TO LIFE
WHILE LIVING WITH LEAVE-TAKING

So far I have dealt with mourning mainly in the context of mourning the loss of a loved one. I believe, however that we experience dying not only in this radical form, but in an endless variety of ways. Whenever we are affected by a loss, whenever separation takes place, there is a need to mourn. Many writers agree that prevented or repressed mourning leads one to see the world as meaningless, one's own existence as worthless and the future as being without hope – reactions of a depressive type occur in consequence. When a loved one dies and we "die" with him, then the mourning process and the emotions that accompany it offer an opportunity to experience ourselves as separate, yet at the same time, as connected in a new way to the history of the deceased. If we evade this mourning process for any reason, we are left behind as individuals who are no longer complete, who are only partly alive. This in turn has an effect upon our self-perception and consequently an effect upon our self-esteem. In this situation it is natural that we withdraw into a symbiotic relationship, into something that existed previously, thus avoiding mourning or altogether avoiding claiming the place in the world that is rightfully ours. In Mitscherlich's book, *The Inability to Mourn,*[79] Loewenfeld's concise formulation is quoted: "...disturbance of this process of mourning will hamper an individual's psychic development, his inter-personal relationships and his spontaneous and creative capabilities."[80] In an article on situations triggering depression, Ute Dieckmann[81] described how a group of analysts who had looked into this question found that "the outbreak of a depression always had to do with a loss which had not been come to terms

123

with." Brown[82] and his co-workers indicate that people who already have low self-esteem cannot cope with loss, because loss reduces their feelings of self-esteem still further. As a result of the poor sense of their own worth, they become depressed. A direct connection between loss and depression is seen only when someone has lost his mother or foster-mother before the eleventh year.

Because death is a reality, we must constantly cope with separation and leave-taking in our lives. Not only must we allow others to die; we must also be prepared to set loved ones free in life, set them free for someone else. We must permit aspects of ourselves to die when the time comes. When the time is past, we must relinquish what we have come to love in our lives. If we do not do this, we remain stuck in the past, thereby shutting ourselves off from the future, and no longer living in the real sense. For this reason we must learn to live for the sake of life, we must "die into life," and learn to deal with this sort of dying.

The breaking off of a relationship without the partner's having died can cause similar despair and can disturb our self-perception in a way similar to a real death. This seems to me to be the most clearly visible in marriage partners who divorce after many years. As with any other loss, all the phases of bereavement are observable in this case: one's self-perception is shaken. The way one experiences the world changes. In this situation, too, where formerly there was relationship, or at least strife, now there is emptiness. The social change is enormous. The social environment is far less willing to grant a divorced individual the right to mourn than it is a widow or widower. He should be happy that "all that" is over now and should stride happily into the future. Some will undoubtedly still find divorce improper and believe that one must suffer the consequences. Not only are divorcees discouraged from mourning, they will be treated with disdain if they indulge in it. And yet, these individuals have also lost their partner. Even when there is the possibility that a friendly relationship with this partner could at some point be reestablished, a marriage relationship is, for most, irretrievably lost. To this is added the feeling of failure, which must also be coped with.

A thirty-eight year old woman divorced her alcoholic husband after twenty years of marriage, simply because she could no longer tolerate the fact that she had to work while he wasted her earnings on alcohol. On top of this, he beat her. When sober, however, he was a very gentle man, ashamed and guilty, who repeatedly promised her a better life. They had no children. After the divorce the woman became increasingly depressed. Her friends found this impossible; they thought she should be happy now that everything was over and done with. But she wasn't happy. The divorce had torn her from her life; she didn't know what she lived for any more. She had only thought about the fact that she could no longer stand life with her husband, but she couldn't stand life without him either.

She spoke of a dream in which her husband died, and she had mourned him bitterly. I told her, her husband had in fact died for her in a certain sense, and we should mourn the loss of this relationship. The woman gladly spoke about her life with this man, describing the many terrible scenes, but also describing the many very happy times. She tended to idealize her husband, which would be compensated at times either by dreams, in which he appeared in a form not at all idealized, or by encounters in reality in which she was forced to acknowledge that she had constructed an ideal image of him. She succeeded in realizing what psychological dynamics had played a role in their relationship: she had basically wanted a weak man, so that she could be the one to help him. She therefore also had guilt feelings and readily submitted to the sadistic impulses of her husband for this reason. We also attempted to understand the husband as her own inner figure, as a characteristic of her own personality.

125

This proved fruitful, though very painful for her. Her life with this man became understandable to her, and in its positive aspects, could be regarded as unique and worthwhile. She also gained insight into the fact that she, too, had a dependent side to her character which reached for help in the form of the bottle or otherwise repressed the pain when disappointment came along. Thus she was able to reconcile herself with this portion of her life and also with the ending of it through divorce. It seems to me important that the mourning process also enabled the woman to realize that what she had experienced with her husband should not, in the future, simply be transferred to all other men. This therapy of course was not only concerned with the mourning process. Light was also shed upon the enormously complex background of her choice of partner.

A dream can forcefully bring home to an individual the need to "die into life." A fifty year old woman sought me out for the first time, "frightened to death" by the following dream:

> *"I am at work in my own business, sitting in my office, and am the manager (as in reality). I open a letter, which is sealed with an old-fashioned seal. In the letter it says that I am sentenced to death. I know that nothing can be done to change this. I am terribly shocked, and quickly begin to organize everything in the business, so that afterwards there will not be too much chaos. Suddenly I lean back, appalled, and think: 'You're going to die tomorrow, and you can think of nothing better to do than to get the business affairs in order.' I wake up filled with the fear of death and horrified at myself that I cannot make use of the time that remains to me."*

The woman told me at the beginning of our discussion of the dream that she had never needed to seek therapy. But since this dream she had felt she must do so, because she was now condemned to death and apparently couldn't do anything about it. The dream seemed to express the fact that she, like all of us, is condemned to die and obviously should give some thought to this. I took the dream as an indication that life does not go on forever. The dreamer had the feeling that the letter had come from another world, that it in any case dealt with something very old-fashioned. I thought of some sort of authority and also considered whether the dream could be expressing aggression that she was directing against herself. The aspect of being threatened in the sense that we are all mortal, given the age of the woman, seemed to make more sense. That death is an old-fashioned thing of course fits – and death is also an authority. Quite naturally the woman was afraid that she was suffering from some incurable illness about which she was unaware, as she seemed in very good health. We then spoke about her being appalled that she had no idea what to do, except to get her business affairs in order. It turned out that this woman lived for her business; everything else came a poor second. She repeatedly formed friendships with people, but because she was more interested in her business than in relationships, these connections remained noncommittal. The woman was shocked to discover that she clearly undervalued so many aspects of life, while attaching to much importance to her business. We agreed that the main thrust of the dream was to call her attention to the fact that she, too, was mortal, that for the moment the immediate change, the consequence of mortality, was that the "manager-only" must die, that in her life other elements needed attention. As I said this, the woman spontaneously formulated ideas as to what she could do: she needed contact with others, with nature, etc. The question of a fatal illness we simply accepted as a possibility which always exists. The woman was not sick at the time, and today (five years after this dream), she is still enjoying good health.

The dream seems to me to be a typical dream, which demands of an individual that she abandon a one-sided attitude, by sacrificing certain aspects of herself, so that other aspects of her personality could develop. Understandably, this could not take place without sadness. Nevertheless, she had to cope with a complete restructuring of her values and get to know herself in situations in which she was significantly less capable. In addition, she had to manage her business in such a way that it could carry on in spite of her other involvements. She was never again to identify with it so much as to become completely symbiotic.

There are dreams that deal even more directly with one's own death. A thirty year old man dreamt:

"I was lying in my bed. The whole family was gathered around me. I thought to myself, I must be dying. I watched myself die. I felt the blood drain from my face and saw how all those around me began to sob. 'So this is the way it is,' I thought, and was content with the family's reaction of grief. Suddenly I saw that I, too, stood at the bedside in the corduroy pants that my mother felt didn't suit me, and I myself observed the way I died. I became confused, began to cry and woke up."

This dream is unusual in that the dream-ego has a double presence as the one who dies, and is even a little proud of it, and as the one who looks on in corduroy trousers. That the dreamer mentioned the corduroy trousers shows that they are significant. In the dream he says that these are the pants that his mother finds unsuitable. These pants might be a way of taking a stand in the world ("wearing the pants") that is unsatisfactory to the mother. The pants were a symbol for making one's own decisions, and were the first pair of pants that he bought against the mother's wishes. The young man in the bed, who has adapted to the mother and is thus accepted within the circle of the family, dies.

In my opinion this dream portrays a personality change. It shows that the analysand likes to occupy center stage and that he has a feeling for the grand exit. Probably it is this desire to be the center of attention, as well as his conformity within the family, down to the detail of the clothing he wears, that must now undergo a radical change. The dream doesn't sound so tragic, and one has the impression that the death cannot have frightened him so much, since he still finds the time to note the quality of his family's mourning. Nevertheless, this must not obscure the fact that the dream has presented the image of death, *the* radical separation, which is accompanied by the fear that overcomes us all when we contemplate death. It could be that, for him, this apparently total change in personality – he needs to do little more – still makes him sad. The dreamer's family was a family that shut itself off from the outside world and cultivated a great deal of contact within itself. Opening up to the outside world was not permitted. This "family vessel" restricted him of course in time. It was, in fact, for the dreamer, as well as for his family, extraordinarily difficult to develop a degree of autonomy. The mother also spoke of the fact that she had "lost her son." The son found himself in a real identity crisis when he no longer identified unquestioningly with the values and viewpoint of his family. Separation was very painful for him.

Such a radical separation can be displayed in other ways in dreams. A thirty-five year old man dreamt:

"It is a funeral service. I am in the church. Mourners are passing by me. I am there with my wife and my three children. My father is somewhere; my brothers are also there with their wives. I look for my mother. I can't see her and inquire about her. Someone tells me she has died; it is for her that the funeral service is being held. She died of a heart attack. I am very sad, but think that that is not a bad way to die."

It happens frequently that the mother or father dies in a dream and must be mourned. It is generally a separation dream indicating that the phase of being the son or the daughter is past. That the mother or father must die usually

129

indicates that, for the son or the daughter involved, the longing for the past is great, and thus an extreme image of separation must be chosen.

This dreamer was a man who was bound closely to his mother. The mother had bound him to her with the threat that she would become sick or even die if he were ever to turn away from her. In spite of this the dreamer had ventured to marry a woman who was not especially to his mother's liking. Since this had also been the case with his brothers, he took no special note of it. When he told me the dream about the mother, he had two years of therapy behind him dealing with anxieties and and problems relating to ambitions and achievements. In the process the problem with his mother had been discussed intensely. It angered him above all that his mother could still unsettle him when she threatened to get sick if he did not come to her on command. When we discussed the dream of the mother's funeral, the dreamer immediately said that, if the dream were true, he would never let himself be blackmailed again and would feel a great deal better. He was astonished at the fact that the death of the mother in the dream had certainly moved him, but it had not "almost killed him," as he had always assumed it would, because of his susceptibility to blackmail. His comment was, "If my mother were not there any more, then we men could finally grow up, and we would have to grow up."

Together we came to the conclusion that the main message of the dream for him was that he could and must be adult.

The dreamer in any case comforted himself with the idea that a sudden death was also a good death. One could ask to what extent he harbored a death wish and simultaneously a bad conscience with respect to his mother, so that he at least let her die a "good" death. This aspect is most certainly contained in the dream. Apart from this, it should be noted that a funeral service is taking place, a collective ritual which was valid for him. I ask myself in that case whether

130

such a ritual could also be essential during such times of transition from the role of "son" to father and husband, since he had emphasized in the dream that he had his family with him. However, the ritual in the dream was concerned less with his initiation into manhood than with the death of the mother. But the two can scarcely be dealt with apart.

Sometimes it happens that parts or aspects of one's personality die and must be buried. A thirty-four year old woman dreamt:

> *"I am in my apartment. Suddenly I hear that Pippi Long-stocking is dead. I am seized by a tremendous feeling of grief. That cannot be true; Pippi Longstocking is immortal. I am completely undone and wake up. I find it peculiar that the death of Pippi Longstocking should affect me so much. I fall asleep again.*
>
> *This time it concerns the fact that Pippi Longstocking must be buried. Someone said that it must be done very cleverly, otherwise she would be certain to rise again from the dead. I asked whether this would really be so bad. The man who spoke, a staid and quiet type, said, 'She endangers marriages and love.' "*

It occurred to the woman that Pippi Longstocking was a very important figure for her, a symbol for a girl who can do absolutely anything, for whom nothing ever goes wrong and who is incredibly cheeky (though it never occurs to anyone to call her cheeky). She is also very soft-hearted and always ready to help, but still, not prepared to be forced into any role as she has a taste for absolute freedom. All this was fascinating for the woman. Her husband, however, found this aspect of her less fascinating. Apart from that, she was not a Pippi Longstocking, and every time she tried to play the Pippi Longstocking, something went wrong.

This aspect of the woman thus died in the dream, and the dreamer is distraught about it. A childish, omnipotent feminine aspect, who plays with everyone and everything, dies;

131

she must abandon this aspect of herself. The seriousness of this is confirmed in the second dream she had on the same night. It is not sufficient that Pippi Longstocking has died, she must now be given back to the earth completely. An even greater separation is demanded than in the first dream. Now it is known that the burial must be done carefully, because there is a great danger that she will come back to life again. This is apparent also in the dreamer's question. She does not think it would be so bad if Pippi Longstocking were to come back to life. But the staid and dignified man believes it would be a bad thing. The dreamer says she does not know this man, but his quiet demeanor pleased her greatly. The man seems to represent an opposite pole to Pippi Longstocking: the protector of marriages and love. For the dreamer what was compelling about the dream was that she had to take leave of her Pippi Longstocking. It was also clear to her that Pippi embodied a very childlike and sometimes childish characteristic. For her the dream carried the feeling that a part of herself had died. She mourned, and approximately three months later, found a Pippi Long-stocking once more in a dream. But this one was much older than the "real" one and preserved, above all, the spontaneity of the real one.

Every major change in our lives can be symbolized by the image of death and sometimes also by the image of rebirth, depending upon which aspect is stressed more. A twenty-two year old woman dreamt on the night before her wedding:

"I go into the church in my bridal gown. No one is there; I become afraid. I am holding the arm of a dark woman; the entire church is in complete darkness. She indicates that I should lie down. I notice that I must lie down in a coffin. I am so afraid, but don't dare to object. I am afraid that they will also bury me. I close my eyes and think: 'I will wait now until Roman [the future husband] comes.' I go to sleep.

132

When I wake up [in the dream], organ music sounds, and I walk on the arm of Roman to the altar. I have the feeling I have slept away a lifetime between yesterday and today."

The dreamer said that she had been very sad in the coffin, that she had experienced a real fear of death, while at the same time having the feeling that there was nothing more to be done about it.

The dream seems to me clearly to indicate that marriage for this woman meant entering into a completely new life situation. The transition is represented by the demand that she should lie in a coffin; she should lie down where the dead belong. In the coffin she falls asleep, later waking up and rising to bind herself to her husband.

The dream can be seen as a psychic initiation into the state of a married woman. The initiation is conducted by a dark woman and takes place in church and coffin, which suggest the sheltering character of the cave, or in the final analysis, the womb of the Great Mother. A great deal of fear is bound up in this initiation. It is especially clear in this dream that an old situation is being left behind, without the new one's as yet being in sight. Roman does not appear before this woman had already accepted possible death.

This dream was dreamt outside therapy and was told by the bride on her wedding day, when she noted that she had apparently underestimated how different her life would now be. I feel the dream indicates that the dreamer must take seriously the fact that a new life phase is beginning, and that she may consciously mourn the ending of the previous phase.

We take leave not only of phases in life, parent figures and aspects of our personalities, we also take leave of ego-ideals and plans for life. Every individual constructs certain ideals during his youth, without being clear as to what is attainable and what is unattainable for him. With neurotic individuals a great gap often opens between the set goals

133

and the real possibilities. The goal of therapy, then, is to bring goals and potential for achievement into a more realistic relationship. This is often a very painful process associated with a great deal of mourning, because one does not achieve what one had anticipated or established as an ideal for oneself.

A thirty year old man had, until now, essentially spent his life acquiring a great deal of knowledge without being able to focus on any sort of professional goal. He felt that one day "all his energies would suddenly focus," all his knowledge would come together in a revelation such as no man had ever had. Now he dreamt:

"Alexander the Great is dead. I am completely over-whelmed by this piece of news, weep, and behave as if I myself had died."

The dreamer was still visibly shaken as he told me this dream. Alexander the Great was a figure with whom he identified. He would have liked to be like him: a philosopher, commander in battle and statesman. In the dreamer's fantasy, Alexander was even endowed with abilities which he might not have possessed in reality. This "greatness" dies in the dream, which undoubtedly meant that this fantasy of greatness, and his identification with this fantasy of greatness, also must die. This was very painful for the dreamer. Certainly he felt relieved of a great burden when he comprehended emotionally that he didn't have to be an Alexander; but at the same time, he felt considerably less significant.

Death always looms in the midst of life. We continually "lose" something, must let go of something, renounce something, separate from one another, give up something. Life continually undergoes change; we must abandon what is familiar and confront change. But we not only lose, we also gain. Precisely because of the many changes, life in its flow presents us with the opportunity to open up and develop as personalities. At the same time, we must leave behind certain aspects of ourselves and learn to experience new aspects. This is not, of course, true abandonment, even when we must separate from a loved one who has died. The life shared with him, the events shared with him are present in our memories, belong to us and constitute part of our lives as well. The experience of mourning for these people is a part of the fabric of our lives; it is also part of us. If we are able to mourn, then it may well be the time when we learn something essential about ourselves.

It seems crucial to me that, through the process of mourning, we learn not only that we can endure separation, but that separation, through mourning, can lead us to a new self-awareness, to a new set of values. We experience ourselves as individuals who do not crumble when confronted with separation, who repeatedly find inner support, who, precisely when shaken, reflect upon what is essential. To experience the death of a loved one is to experience one of life's extreme events. It effects *us*. No one else can experience it for us. For this reason it is a moment which we can experience demanding existence between life's greatest opposites. Even if death is unavoidable and accompanies us constantly, our life, our relationships and our histories are just as certain as death.

Death looms in life in the form of constant change. Life in the face of death must be lived in the "readiness to take leave." We must always be prepared to bid farewell, to undergo change, and also must always be prepared to perceive our life story as being a story of unending change, as the unfolding of our identity.

Weischedel[83] writes, "The ability to take leave is the fitting answer of the skeptic (one for whom everything is questionable – my remark) to the spectacle of transience, which determines and controls everything real."[84]

By "the ability to take leave," Weischedel means to take leave continuously from that in which one tends to linger.[85] He refers to a double leave-taking: a leave-taking with respect to oneself and a leave-taking with respect to the world. Weischedel views the readiness to take leave as an attitude essential to the individual in view of the fact that we all must die. He is of the opinion that the "ability to take leave" requires that an individual constantly maintain a distance between himself and the world.

The idea of an ability to live with the necessity to take leave and the thought of a constant transformation certainly appeals to me. It also seems obvious that, to the "ability to take leave," also belongs the ability to achieve a certain distance to the world. Nevertheless, I am just as convinced that the constant maintenance of a distance to life, because death exists, is not justified. Without the readiness to become involved in relationships, separation and the necessity to take leave are superfluous. Also, when Weischedel says that the individual who lives in the readiness to take leave will dream no dreams of eternity and immortality,[86] this seems in no way to be certain. It appears rather to be a dream of his own. Here, at the very least, he departs from the level of the open question, which is the premise upon which his conclusions are based. As a skeptic he must leave this open and available to question. Precisely at the point when we take the necessity to "take leave" seriously, the longing for "permanence," for symbiosis, for something which endures, will make itself felt in the individual. Even if I perceive myself as a constantly developing individual and know that I will undergo change any number of times, I will nevertheless never experience myself as anyone other than "myself," except in a pathological condition. For me the experience of identity is supposed to be something certain, but in view of separation, I also feel that the individual's need for relationship is not to be ignored. There is not only death, there is also love.

If leave-taking is demanded so radically, then relationships must also be important, and over and above this, it must be important for the individual to know he is sustained. It may be that, in the course of life, he has learned to introject a supportive and accepting environment as something that arises out of his own personality. It may be that he experiences his psyche as something transcendent with which he can be symbiotic, thereby enhancing life. The individual who has trust in further relationships is able to separate. He who always knows that there is a place where he can find peace can live in the ability to take leave. The image of the nomad symbolizes this: the nomad is always moving on, but also always settles down again for a time. That which he needs in life he carries with him.

To exist always in the readiness to take leave is difficult for us. It is difficult for us to have to accept separation repeatedly. We defend ourselves against change, attempt to deny it, even where it has long since taken place. Do we defend ourselves against death? Against death's intrusion into the midst of life? Coming to a standstill means, precisely, death. In order not to have to see death, we deny it and its companion, change – and then all of a sudden we are dead. Becker[87] writes:

> *"The human being must pay with his life. Every day he must be ready to die, to expose himself to the risks and dangers of this world and let himself be devoured and consumed by them. Otherwise in the end he is as if dead, because he was desperately trying to run away from life as he runs from death. Modern existentialist psychiatrists interpret depression in this way."*

Becker is referring to Médard Boss.[88] When one is not prepared to live in the readiness to take leave, to incorporate death into life, then depression threatens. Becker also makes a connection between the inability to endure loss and change and a tendency towards depression. Life requires the repeated sacrifice of what we think we are and what we think we have achieved, so that something new may again enter into life. But we must also have the certainty that existence can be built up again; that, in spite of constant change, we can be creative and that these changes are an aspect of creativity. However, we also need the feeling of a continuity of identity in order to have the courage to achieve distance to ourselves and trustingly allow the unknown to approach us.

I would like to define identity as a feeling of being at one with oneself as a developed and developing individual, who forms himself ever anew, because his ego is receptive inwardly and outwardly. Each new development is an addition to what already exists, a new potential for action upon which one can rely. Identity assumes a relationship to oneself, to one's body, to one's soul and to one's environment. Relationships to others, our bonds, are an essential aspect of our identity that I would like to call our "relational identity," because it assumes relatedness in many forms and also makes one capable of relationships.[89]

The ability to live in the readiness to take leave requires a relationship to ourselves and to a transcendental background in us by which we feel supported. It requires the knowledge that we possess the capability for commitment to others whom we trust, as well as the faith in our own ability to structure our existence. Is it astonishing that we prefer not to have to live in the readiness to take leave, even though life then turns against us? Of course, there is also the opposite philosophy of life: death is certain in any case, so we let life slip away from us. Nothing is then really important; everything is transient. The construction of one's own existence is no longer attractive.

Defense against transiency can take many forms; for instance, "activity in the face of death," which Scheler[90] emphatically outlines with his theory that the individual has replaced belief in an eternal life with progress for the sake of progress. Other forms of resistance can be seen in the attempt to overcome death and the hope that one day we really will conquer it. We can refuse to engage in life at all, preferring to remain stationary at a childlike stage of development. Another possibility is identification with death as the "indestructible destroyer." I would like to look at this aspect of defense against mortality, as well as the tendency to devalue everything which has to do with life.

Mary Williams[91] proposes the interesting theory that sado-masochism can be seen as a "method" of dealing with the fear of death. She sees in sadism a contra-phobic (fear-banishing) identification with death as destroyer. The victim is mortal, the perpetrator can participate in the ecstasy of immortality. The sadist identifies with death as "the indestructible destroyer" and projects mortality onto the victim. The masochist identifies with the mortal victim and projects invincibility onto the other, the rescuer, who will redeem him from mortality. Williams sees in masochism a contra-phobic reaction to unconscious sadism. She labels sadism and masochism the most perverted of behavior patterns.

Williams' theory stands to reason. There remains, of course, the question as to what conditions cause an individual to develop the need to identify with the "indestructible destroyer" in order to be able to tolerate the thought of mortality. This must be an individual with an identity crisis, presumably due to separations with which he has been unable to cope. Sadists generally suffer from an extreme fear of powerlessness which they compensate with power behavior. Confronted with death, we all are powerless in the end. The temptation to identify with the "indestructible destroyer" is close to us all.

It seems to me that Williams' theory is extremely useful with respect to therapy involving individuals with a strong sadistic super-ego streak. If death is hidden behind this sadistic super-ego streak, then the personal problem becomes a general human problem; the problem becomes extremely serious. I ask myself to what extent destructiveness in general has its source in such an identification with death as destroyer.

With the reference to sado-masochism as a behavior mode, Williams raised the whole problem of the repression of death in relationships. She postulates that where there is a strong repression of death by both partners, sado-masochistic behavior can arise, whereby one plays the role of the destroyer and the other the destroyed. The roles are presumably interchangeable.

Willi[92] ascertained that the "anal-sadistic collusion" represents the most common form of marriage conflict in our society (the author is Swiss – translator's note). The sado-masochistic collusion is an aspect of this. By "collusion" Willi refers to an interaction between partners who have a basic unresolved conflict of the same type. According to Williams' theory, this would be the repression of death. The partners play their roles as if one actually complements the other. In fact, each role is just a variation of the other, usually a polarized variation. In our example: both are concerned with mortality and immortality. The sadist identifies with the "indestructible destroyer" and projects mortality onto the victim, with the victim playing the opposite role. The basic problem is the same. However, because the basic problem is the same, it can happen that the behavior pattern of the one partner (even if he had strictly excluded the possibility for himself in the hope that, in this way, the other might "redeem" him from the basic conflict) reveals itself as his own behavior potential, precisely because it has been repressed for so long. Then the fantasy of mutual redemption cannot be maintained any longer. One must then work on the underlying conflict which, in this case, arises from the fact of mortality and the wish for immortality.

The sado-masochistic collusion concerns dominance and submission, power, possession, using and being used. It poses the question as to whether Williams' theory might be broadened to encompass all authority problems, all problems concerning power. It is interesting that Wilke[93] proposes the thesis that, in the analysis of individuals who suffer from problems pertaining to authority, a discussion of death and mortality is of particular importance. The experience that no authority is exempt from death helps us to see authority in relative terms; the experience that one is oneself also mortal helps one to see oneself in relative terms. Power as a struggle against mortality, to understand it in the end as the attempt to identify with death, could explain why the striving for power is so strong. It could also explain why the loss of power cuts so deep. Power and "living with the necessity to take leave" are incompatible, since the goal of power is possession and the keeping of what has been won. When power is conceptualized as opposing the necessity to live in the readiness to take leave, then we lose when we lose power. We lose not only influence, money and so forth, but we are reminded that life is transient and that no "defense against death" is guaranteed.

I see devaluing – be it the devaluing of oneself, the world or life itself – in the same context. It seems to me to be the regressive form of the attempt to gain power over others or even power over the world and life. In devaluing others and the world, one becomes powerful oneself. It is not the competitive, active form of power acquisition; it is a form of power that lays a veil of worthlessness over oneself and others. Behind this form of power also lies an identification with death as the destroyer. But this form of power also contains the problem that the new opportunities presented as a consequence of human mortality cannot be accepted. If this aspect of living in the readiness to take leave is perceived only as painful loss, our transitory nature lies like frost over our lives. Everything becomes banal and relative. The opposite of devaluing, idealizing, has the same roots. If an awareness that everything is transient lies behind devaluing, without the positive consequences' being drawn from this (in other words, without really living in the readiness to take leave and thereby avoiding the temptation to perceive life as banal), then the awareness that life is transient lies behind idealization in the same way. In this case there will be a desperate attempt to invest everyone and everything with a significance that is undeserved. Through "significance" the fear of amounting to nothing is at least temporarily relieved.

Considering the ways in which we defend ourselves against death, it becomes clear that living in the readiness to take leave, as is appropriate to a life that has its limits, instills in us a great fear. It causes us to search for some position for ourselves that is "certain," even to the point of identifying death as the "indestructible destroyer." In this it can be seen once again how much a fusion with something transcendent is sought. In fusion with death as the indestructible destroyer, the fusion occurs with only *one* aspect of death, with the aspect of the "destroyer." Thus death is essentially robbed of its transcendental quality and is reduced to something comprehensible. The longing for symbiosis with something transcendent might be evoked by this fusion with death as destroyer, but because death has been "reduced," the experience of the symbiosis cannot be one of liberation. For this reason symbiosis with death can provide a feeling of "power," but not a feeling of life enhancement or of security. The resulting attitude to life (sado-masochism, for example) carries death within it, with a preference for violence and all that is lifeless.

Erich Fromm[94] speaks in this connection of necrophilia as an orientation which does not love the living, but the dead: not growth, but destruction:

"Necrophilia is a fundamental orientation; it is precisely the answer to life which stands in complete opposition to life. It is the most morbid and most dangerous of the life orientations of which the human being is capable. It is a genuine perversion: although one lives, one does not love the living, but rather, the dead; not growth, but destruction. When the necrophiliac ventures to be true to his feelings, then he expresses the motto of his life with the words, 'Long live death.' "

If we consider how many depressive individuals suffer under their sadistic super-egos, then we must see the increase in depressive illness as evidence of a partial identification with death as destroyer.

The problem of fusion with death as the indestructible destroyer is that the creative forces which stand in opposition cannot be used. Fromm sets the biophilous orientation in opposition to the necrophilous orientation of an individual. The biophiliac is the individual who loves life, who chooses to risk the adventure in life rather than look for security. Of course, no one is either exclusively necrophilous or biophilous. To be only biophilous would mean that death is again excluded. Quite apart from this, many creative achievements are accompanied by destruction. So that new values can be brought into being, old values are destroyed, both in the collective and in the individual experience.

When we live creatively, we take into account the acceptance of change, the endurance of uncertainty, the ability to "let go" in the face of death. We await new ideas and link these to the familiar so that the familiar is either expanded or must be regarded in a new way. These are fundamental aspects of the creative attitude, but they are also essential aspects of the art of living in general.[95]

It is therefore not astonishing that, for Jung, the goal of therapy is the instilling of the creative attitude in the individual.[96] But also other therapists, Rogers,[97] for example, and Landau, lay great store by creativity in therapy.

Gordon in her book, *Dying and Creating,*[98] is right when she proposes the idea that the psychological attitude which enables a good death is precisely the attitude that encourages creative work. It is an attitude which accepts the necessity to separate repeatedly from what is familiar, mourns and trusts that something new will result.

Death as a problem is important in every therapy. Our relationship to death, our fears, our defense mechanisms, our images of death, the symbolic significance that it has in general, and the symbolic significance with which we invest it, greatly influences our lives. This is presumably also true from a collective perspective. Dunne[99] proposes that the Egyptian culture was able to exist so long and with such stability because the concept of death was in no way repressed. One lived constantly with the thought of death, in the expectation of help from the gods and in the hope of a good life in the Hereafter.

But when we discuss death, we must also discuss mourning. Mourning for an individual whom we loved is an extreme case in which death intrudes into our lives, and the changes it brings are experienced most keenly. Self-perception and our perception of the world collapse, and it becomes clear how much "living in the readiness to take leave" is demanded of us – and how much pain this causes. But this extreme case also shows us that separations, as difficult as they are, do not only mean loss, but are a challenge to the greatest possible self-realization. Dealing with the loss will be aided by dreams. After the termination of a mourning process, an individual can enter into a new relationship, well aware of the fact that death can take a loved one again at any time.

This extreme case of loss, this extreme encounter with death, can make us aware of our everyday encounters with death. Perhaps it shows us that we must change, or must accept loss. Death is not a one-off event; it is always present in our lives demanding change. Living in the readiness to take leave is the answer to this. Part of this readiness to take leave is a knowledge of our own history and our innermost identity, the knowledge that we can experience unity and continuity in the symbiosis with something transcendent; in the end, the knowledge that we can confront transiency with a creative attitude.

It seems to me that mourning is also important in our everyday encounters with death. If we don't acknowledge this then we underestimate death's importance and the pain it inflicts. Through the emotion of mourning we can become healthy, as paradoxical as this sounds, for mourning brings about transformation.

We can see death as that power which constantly drives us to transform. The thought of transformation can be a fascinating thought, but the price of transformation is separation, loss. If we overlook this, particularly in psychotherapy, where we are so much concerned with transformation, then transformation is unlikely to take place. Only mourning can bring about transformation; it enables us to really take leave and prepares the individual for new relationships.

FOOTNOTES

Translations of titles and titles available in English, where these were obtainable, have been provided in the Bibliography.

1 A. Augustinus, *Confessiones III*, 4, 9; 6, 11; Dreizehn Bücher Bekenntnisse, translated by Carl Johann Perl, annotated by Adolf Holl. 2nd edit., Paderborn 1964, p. 77 ff.
2 E. Lindemann, "The Symptomatology and Management of Acute Grief," *American Journal of Psychiatry*, 101, 1944, p. 144.
3 C.M. Parkes, *Vereinsamung. Die Lebenskrise bei Partnerverlust* (Hamburg: Rowohlt Taschenbuch 7130, 1978).
4 J. Bowlby, *Loss, Sadness and Depression* (London: Hogarth Press, 1980), p. 151 f.
   Bowlby reported an investigation of 60 persons who had lost their partners. The investigation was conducted three years after the death event. One person had committed suicide during this time.
5 Cf. F. Wiplinger, *Der personal verstandene Tod* (Freiburg: Alber, 1980).
6 G. Marcel, *Gegenwart und Unsterblichkeit* (Frankfurt a. M.: Verlag Knecht, 1961), p. 287.
7 Parkes, *op. cit.*
8 The shiva: the seven days of mourning which are observed following the death of a relative, during which one sits in the home of the deceased, prays, speaks of the deceased and takes over all reponsibilities for the bereaved, simply letting him or her feel warmth and comfort.
9 R. Kuhn, quoted in Parkes, *op. cit.*, p. 115.
10 H.J. Schultz (ed.), *Einsamkeit* (Stuttgart: Kreuz Verlag, 1980).
11 Cf. also Parkes, *op. cit.*, p. 77.
12 E. Kübler-Ross, *Interviews mit Sterbenden* (Stuttgart: Kreuz Verlag, 1980).
   In this book Kübler-Ross describes five phases which an individual goes through upon learning that he suffers from a terminal illness:
   1st Phase: Denial and Isolation
   2nd Phase: Anger
   3rd Phase: Bargaining
   4th Phase: Depression
   5th Phase: Acceptance
   Kübler-Ross describes the phase of depression thus: the individual takes leave and mourns, because he must take leave of so many. These stages described by Kübler-Ross seem to me also to apply to the process of mourning undergone by those left behind.
13 Cf. Parkes, *op. cit.*, p. 55 ff.
   Bowlby, *op. cit.*, p. 85.
14 Schelling, Brief über den Tod Carolines vom 2. Oktober 1809 an Immanuel Niethammer, ed. by J.L. Döderlein, Stuttgart-Bad Cannstadt, 1975. Quoted in: G. Scherer, *Das Problem des Todes in der Philosophie*

(Darmstadt: Wissenschaftliche Buchgesellschaft, 1979), p. 79.
15 G. Marcel, *op. cit.*, p. 238.
    Kritik dieser Aussage: F. Wiplinger, *op. cit.*, p. 102 ff.
16 Cf., for example, Bowlby, *op. cit.*, p. 85.
    Cf., for example, Parkes, *op. cit.*, p. 203.
17 Kübler-Ross, *op. cit.*
18 Cf., for example, S. Freud, *Trauer und Melancholie*. In: Psychologie des
    Unbewußten. Sudienausgabe Vol III. Conditio Humana (Frankfurt a. M.:
    Fischer, 1975) p. 194 ff.
    Cf. Parkes, *op. cit.*, in various places, for example, p. 216.
    Cf. J.E. Meyer, *Todesangst und das Todesbewußtsein der Gegenwart*
    (Berlin: Springer, 1979), p. 55.
19 Cf. Parkes, *op. cit.*, p. 75.
    Parkes mentions that widows who had dreams in which they met again
    with their partners had significantly fewer sleep disturbances than those
    who did not have these dreams or fantasies.
20 Cf. Bowlby, *op. cit.*, for example, p. 151, 182.
21 H. Kasack, *Die Stadt hinter dem Strom* (Frankfurt: Suhrkamp, 1972).
22 Jung on interpretation on the objective and subjective levels: "When I
    speak of interpreting a dream or fantasy on the objective level, I mean that
    the persons or situations appearing in it are referred to objectively real
    persons or situations, in contrast to interpretation on the subjective level
    ... where the persons or situations appearing in it refer to subjective
    factors entirely belonging to the subject's own psyche." *Psychological
    Types*, Volume 6, par. 779, par. 812.
23 Parkes, *op. cit.*, p. 78.
24 Freud describes the process of mourning: "In what now does the work
    which mourning performs consist? ... Reality-testing has shown that the
    loved object no longer exists and it proceeds to demand that all libido shall
    be withdrawn from its attachment to that object ... Each single one of the
    memories and expectations in which the libido is bound to the object is
    brought up and hyper-cathected in respect of it." translation taken from S.
    Freud, The Complete Psychological Works, *Mourning and Melancholia,*
    Vol. XIV, p. 244. (London: Hogarth Press, 1966-1974).
    Paula Heimann said regarding the concept of the mourning process:
    "Level by level, step by step, the mourner recalls his experiences with the
    loved object under the dictates of the reality that he has lost this object,
    that such experiences are no more to be had. Thus, remembering becomes
    a stepwise, continuous rending of the bond to the loved object and
    therefore an experience of tearing and wounding in the self of the
    mourner. In the mourning process the pain of all previous losses will be
    repeated ... in order to oppose the temptation not to submit to the painful
    mourning task and die bound to the object, a healthy narcissism is
    required, as a result of which remaining in life and joy of living possess a
    high value and are the reward for going through the mourning process." P.
    Heimann, "Bemerkungen zum Arbeitsbegriff in der Psychoanalyse," in
    Psyche 20, 1966, p. 321 ff.
25 M. Scheler, *Tod und Fortleben*, Ges. Werke, Vol. 10, Schriften aus dem
    Nachlass, Vol. 1, Bern, 1957.
26 Bowlby, *op. cit.*
    Parkes, *op. cit.*

27 Kübler-Ross, *op. cit.*, p. 99 f.
28 Bowlby, *op. cit.*
29 Bowlby, *op. cit.*, p. 85.
30 Parkes, *op. cit.*, p. 203.
31 Parkes, *op. cit.*
    Bowlby, *op. cit.*, p. 90.
32 S. Grof, J. Halifax, *Die Begegnung mit dem Tod* (Stuttgart: Klett/Cotta, 1980), p. 157.
33 Cf. Ph. Aries, *Geschichte des Todes* (Munich: Hauser, 1980), p. 24 ff.
34 G. Gorer, *Death, Grief and Mourning* (London: Camelot Press, 1965).
35 Parkes, *op. cit.*, p. 63 f.
36 G.W. Brown, T. Harris, J.R. Copeland, "Depression and Loss," *British Journal of Psychiatry,* 130, 1977, pp. 1-18.
37 Parkes, *op. cit.*, for example, p. 50.
38 V. Kast, *Das Assoziationsexperiment in der therapeutischen Praxis* (Fellbach/Stuttgart: Bonz, 1980), p. 15 ff.
39 C.G. Jung, "Die transzendente Funktion." In *Dynamik des Unbewußten,* GW8 (Rascher: Zürich, 1967), p. 91. (Collected Works Vol. 8, *The Structure and Dynamics of the Psyche,* "The Transcendent Function," par. 159.)
40 Cf. Parkes, *op. cit.*, p. 77.
    Bowlby, *op. cit.*, p. 97...
    Gorer, *op. cit.*
41 Parkes, *op. cit.*, p. 187.
42 Freud, *op. cit.*
43 Freud, *op. cit.*, p. 199.
44 E. Jacobson, *Depression* (Frankfurt: Suhrkamp, 1977).
45 Jacobson, *op. cit.*, p. 123.
46 H. Deutsch, "Absence of Grief," *Psychoanalytic Quarterly,* 6, 1937, pp. 12-22.
47 Cf., for example, studies of V. Volkan, "Typical Findings in Pathological Grief," *Psychiatric Quarterly,* 44, 1970, pp.231-250.
48 Bowlby, *op. cit.*, p. 153.
49 Cf. W. Schmiedbauer, *Die hilflosen Helfer* (Hamburg: Rowohlt, 1977).
50 G. Szonn, "Trauerarbeit mit dem Katathymen Bilderleben," in H. Leuner (ed.), *Katathymes Bilderleben* (Bern/Stuttgart: Huber, 1980), pp. 263-271.
    "Katathymic Image Association," developed by H. Leuner, is a procedure which makes use of the daydream, whereby the participant will be asked in a relaxed state to give himself over to a certain imagination in association with a given image and to give his fantasy free rein to develop. The one fantasizing is for the most part intensely involved in this. The more relaxed the participant is, the more colorful and lively become his fantasies, and the more powerful his emotional involvement is. Leuner and his co-workers use standard motifs, such as the meadow, the brook, etc. These motifs can of course be expanded, as Szonn did in working with the woman who could not mourn.
51 Parkes, *op. cit.*, p. 91.
52 Parkes, *op. cit.*, pp. 190-193.
53 Cf. R. Lord, S. Ritvo, A.J. Solnit, "Patients' Reaction to the Death of the Psychoanalyst," *International Journal of Psycho-Analysis,* 59, 1978, p. 189.

149

54 C.M. Parkes, B. Benjamin, R.G. Fitzgerald, "Broken Heart: A Statistical Study of Increased Mortality Among Widowers," *British Medical Journal*, 1, 1969, pp. 740-743.
55 Brown, Harris, Copeland, *op. cit.*
   The investigation is discussed in detail in Bowlby, *op. cit.*, pp. 250-262.
55a In: Finnische und Estnische Märchen, *Märchen der Weltliteratur* (Köln-Düsseldorf: Diederichs-Verlag, 1962).
56 V. Volkan, "A Study of a Patient's 'Re-Grief' Work," *Psychiatric Quarterly*, 45/1, 1971, pp. 255-273.
57 Cf. Volkan, *op. cit.*
   Bowlby, *op. cit.*
   Brown, Harris, Copeland, *op. cit.*
58 M. Mahler, *Symbiose und Individuation* (Stuttgart: Klett, 1972), p. 14.
59 M. Mahler, F. Pine, A. Bergman, *Die psychische Geburt des Menschen* (Frankfurt a. M.: Fischer, 1978).
60 Simone de Beauvoir, *Une mort très douce* (Paris: Gallimard, 1964).
61 St. Paul, Letter to the Philippians 1, 23-24.
62 Teresa von Avila, Vita 24,7.
63 H. Kohut, *Narzissmus* (Frankfurt: Suhrkamp, 1973).
   H. Kohut, *Die Heilung des Selbst* (Frankfurt: Suhrkamp, 1979).
   O. Kernberg, *Borderline Störungen und pathologischer Narzissmus* (Frankfurt: Suhrkamp, 1978).
64 Meyer, *op. cit.*, p. 34.
65 Meyer, *ibid.*
66 G. Bataille, *Der heilige Eros* (Darmstadt: Luchterhand, 1963).
67 The theme love and death dominates, for example, the work of Ingeborg Bachmann.
   Ingeborg Bachmann, *Werke.* ed. by Ch. Koschel, J. von Weidenbaum, C. Münster (München: Piper, 1978). Condensed in the 15th Lied of "Lieder auf der Flucht," Vol. 1, p. 147.
68 R.M. Rilke, *Werke in 3 Bänden* (Frankfurt: Insel Verlag, 1966), Vol 1, p. 233.
69 Meyer, *op. cit.*, p. 49.
70 C.G. Jung, *Psychologische Typen* (Zürich: Rascher, 1960), p. 512 ff. (Collected Works Vol. 6, *Psychological Types,* par. 789.).
71 Grof and Halifax, *op. cit.*, p. 155.
72 *Ibid.*
73 Cf. C.G. Jung, *Mysterium Coniunctionis,* GW 14/1 and 14/2, in particular 14/2 (Zürich: Rascher, 1968), p. 324 ff. (Collected Works Vol. 14, *Mysterium Coniunctionis,* par. 776.).
74 Cf. Mahler, *op. cit.*
75 Cf. O. Rank, *Beyond Psychology* (New York: Dover Publications, 1958), p. 1196. First published in 1941.
76 Brown, Harris, Copeland, *op. cit.*
77 Cf. Fairy tales of the grateful dead, for example, "Rothaarig-Grünäugig," in *Märchen aus Kurdistan,* Märchen der Weltliteraturk (Köln-Düsseldorf: Diederichs-Verlag, 1978).
78 *Das Gilgamesh-Epos* (Stuttgart: Reclam, 1958).
79 A. and M. Mitscherlich, *Die Unfähigkeit zu trauern* (München: Piper, 1967).
80 Mitscherlich, *op. cit.*, p. 9.

81 U. Dieckmann, "Ein archetypischer Aspekt in der auslösenden Situation der Depression," *Analytische Psychologie* 5, 1974, pp. 97-112.
82 Brown, Harris, Copeland, *op. cit.*
83 W. Weischedel, *Skeptische Ethik* (Frankfurt: Suhrkamp, 1980).
84 *Op. cit.,* p. 196.
85 *Op. cit.,* p. 194.
86 *Op. cit.,* p. 196.
87 E. Becker, *Die Dynamik des Todes* (Olten: Walter, 1976), p. 310.
88 M. Boss, *Psychoanalyse und Daseinsanalytik* (Bern: Huber, 1957).
89 Taken in abbreviated form from V. Kast, "Weibliche Werte im Umbruch - Konsequenzen für die Partnerschaft," *Analytische Psychologie* 10, 1979, pp. 133-151.
90 Scheler, *op. cit.*
91 M. Williams, "The Fear of Death," *Journal of Analytical Psychology,* 3, 1958, pp. 157-165.
92 J. Willi, *Die Zweierbeziehung* (Hamburg: Rowohlt, 1975), p. 107. Summary discussion of collusion, p. 59 f.
93 H.J. Wilke, "Autoritätskomplex und autoritäre Persönlichkeitsstruktur," *Analytische Psychologie* 8, 1977, pp. 33-40.
94 E. Fromm, *Die Seele des Menschen* (Stuttgart: Deutsche Verlagsanstalt, 1979), p. 41.
95 R. Gordon, *Dying and Creating. A Search for Meaning* (London: The Society of Analytical Psychology, 1978).
96 C.G. Jung, *Praxis der Psychotherapie* GW 16 (Olten: Walter, 1971), p. 49. (Collected Works Vol. 16, *The Practice of Psychotherapy,* par. 82).
97 C.R. Rogers, "Towards a Theory of Creativitiy," in *Creativity and its Cultivation,* ed. H. Anderson (New York: McGraw Hilll, 1959).
98 Gordon, *op. cit.*
99 J.S. Dunne, *The City of the Gods* (London: Sheridan Press, 1974).

BIBLIOGRAPHY

Abraham, K., (Psychoanalytical Studies II) *Psychoanalytische Studien II*, Frankfurt a. M.: Fischer, 1971.

Anderson, H., *Creativity and its Cultivation*, New York: McGraw Hill, 1959.

Apostel Paulus, (Epistle to the Philippians) *Brief an die Philipper*, 1, 23 f.

Ariès, Ph., (The Hour of our Death) *Geschichte des Todes*, München: Hauser, 1980.

Augustinus, A., (Confessions) *Confessiones III*, 4, 9; 6, 11, Dreizehn Bücher Bekenntnisse, translated by Carl Johan Perl, annotated by Adolf Holl, 2nd edition, Paderborn, 1964.

Bataille, G., (Holy Eros) *Der heilige Eros*, Darmstadt: Luchterhand, 1963.

Beauvoir, S. de, (A Very Easy Death) *Une mort très douce*, Paris: Gallimard, 1964.

Becker, E., (The Dynamics of Death) *Die Dynamic des Todes*, Olten: Walter, 1976.

Boros, L., (The Mystery of Death) *Mysterium Mortis*, Olten: Walter, 1962.

Boss, M., (Psychoanalysis and Existential Philosophy) *Psychoanalyse und Daseinsanalytik*, Bern: Huber, 1957.

Bowlby, J., (Separation; Anxiety and Anger) *Trennung*, Munich: Kindler, 1976.

Bowlby, J., *Loss; Sadness and Depression*, London: Hogarth Press, 1980.

Brown, G.W., Harris, T., Copeland, J.R., "Depression and Loss," *British Journal of Psychiatry* 130, 1977, pp. 1-18.

Deutsch, H., "Absence of Grief," *Psychoanalytic Quarterly*, 6, 1937, pp. 12-22.

Dieckmann, U., (An Archetypal Aspect of a Situation Triggering Depression) "Ein archetypischer Aspekt in der auslösenden Situation der Depression," *Analytische Psychologie*. 5, 1974, pp. 97-112.

Döderlein, J.L. (ed.), (Schelling's letter on the death of his wife, Caroline, to Immanuel Niethammer; Quoted in G. Schwerer, The Problem of Death in Philosophy) Brief Schellings über den Tod seiner Frau Caroline an Immanuel Niethammer; Stuttgart/Bad-Cannstadt, 1975; cit. in: G. Schwerer, *Das Problem des Todes in der Philosophie*, Darmstadt: Wissenschaftliche Buchgesellschaft, 1979.

Dunne, J.S., *The City of Gods*, London: Sheridan Press, 1974.

Feifel, H. (ed.), *The Meaning of Death*, New York: McGraw Hill, 1959, 1965.

Franz, M.L. von, Frey-Rohn, L., Jaffé, A., (Concerning Death) *Im Umkreis des Todes*, Zürich: Daimon Verlag, 1980. (English edition in preparation.)

Freud, S., (Mourning and Melancholia) *Trauer und Melancholie;* in: Psychologie des Unbewußten, Studienausgabe Bd. III; Conditio Humana, Frankfurt: Fischer, 1975.

Fromm, E., (The Heart of Man) *Die Seele des Menschen*, Stuttgart: Deutsche Verlagsanstalt, 1979.

Gilgmesch-Epos, Stuttgart: Reclam, 1958.

Gordon, R., *Dying and Creating. A Search for Meaning*, London: The Society of Analytical Psychology, 1978.

Gorer, G., *Death, Grief and Mourning*, London: Camelot Press, 1965.

Grof, S., Halifax, J., (The Human Encounter with Death) *Die Begegnung mit dem Tod*, Stuttgart: Klett/Cotta, 1980.

Heimann, P., (Remarks on a Working Concept in Psychoanalysis) "Bemerkungen zum Arbeitsbegriff in der Psychoanalyse," *Psyche*, 20, 1960, p. 321 ff.

Herzog, E., (Psyche and Death) *Psyche und Tod*, Zürich: Rascher, 1960.

Jacobson, E., *Depression*, Frankfurt: Suhrkamp, 1977.

Jung, C.G., ("The Theory of Psychoanalysis," Freud and Psychoanalysis, The Collected Works of C.G. Jung, Vol. 4) "Versuch einer Darstellung der psychoanalytischen Theory," *Jahrbuch für Psychoanalytische und Psychopathologische Forschung*, Band V, 1913, Zürich: Rascher, 1955.

Jung, C.G., (Psychological Types, The Collected Works of C.G. Jung, Volume 6) *Psychologische Typen*, GW6, Zürich: Rascher, 1921.

Jung, C.G., (The Practice of Psychotherapy. The Collected Works of C.G. Jung, Volume 16) *Praxis der Psychotherapie*, GW16, Olten: Walter, 1957, 1971.

Jung, C.G., ("The Transcendent Function" in The Structure and Dynamics of the Psyche, The Collected Works of C.G. Jung, Volume 8) "Die transzendente Funktion," in *Dynamik des Unbewußten*, GW8, Zürich: Rascher, 1967.

Jung, C.G., (Mysterium Coniunctionis, The Collected Works of C.G. Jung, Volume 12) *Mysterium Coniunctionis*, GW14/1 und GW14/2, Zürich: Rascher, 1968.

Kasack, H., (The City Beyond the River) *Die Stadt hinter dem Strom*, Frankfurt: Suhrkamp, 1947, 1972.

Kast, V., (Upheaval in Feminine Values - Consequences for Partnership) "Weibliche Werte im Umbruch - Konsequenzen für die Partnerschaft," *Analytische Psychologie*, 10, 1979, pp. 133-151.

Kast, V., (The Association Experiment in Therapeutic Practice) *Das Assoziationsexperiment in der therapeutischen Praxis*, Fellbach / Stuttgart: Bonz, 1980.

Kernberg, O., (Borderline Conditions and Pathological Narcissism) *Borderline Störungen und pathologischer Narzissmus*, Frankfurt: Suhrkamp, 1978.

Kohut, H., (Narcissism) *Narzissmus*, Frankfurt: Suhrkamp, 1973.

Kohut, H., (The Restoration of the Self) *Die Heilung des Selbst*, Frankfurt: Suhrkamp, 1979.

Koschel, Ch., von Weidenbaum, J., Münster, C. (ed.), Ingeborg Bachmann (Works) *Werke*, Munich: Piper, 1978.

Kübler-Ross, E., (Interviews with the Dying) *Interviews mit Sterbenden*, Stuttgart: Kreuz Verlag, 13th Edit., 1980.

Landau, E., (Psychology of Creativity) *Psychologie der Kreativität*, Munich/Basel: Reinhardt-Verlag, 1969.

Landau, E., (Assisting the Dying with Katathymic Image Association) "Sterbehilfe mit dem Katathymen Bilderleben," In H. Leunder (ed.), *Katathymes Bilderleben*, Bern/Stuttgart: Huber, 1980.

Leuenbergerr, R., (Death) *Der Tod*, Zürich: Theologischer Verlag, 1971.

Leuner, H., (Katathymic Image Association) *Katathymes Bilderleben*, Bern/Stuttgart: Huber, 1980.

Lindemann, E., "The Symptomatology and Management of Acute Grief." *American Journal of Psychiatry*, 101, 1944, p. 144.

Lord, R., Ritvo, S., Solnit, A.J., "Patients' Reaction to the Death of the Psychoanalyst," 59, 1978, p. 189.

Mahler, M., (On Human Symbiosis and the Vicissitudes of Individuation) *Symbiose und Individuation*, Stuttgart: Klett, 1972.

Mahler, M., Pine, F., Bergman, A., (The Psychic Birth of the Human Infant) *Die psychische Geburt des Menschen,* Frankfurt a. M.: Fischer, 1978.

Marcel G., (The Present and Immortality) *Gegenwart und Unsterblichkeit,* Frankfurt a. M.: Verlag Knecht, 1961.

(Fairy Tales from Kurdistan) *Märchen aus Kurdistan,* Märchen der Weltliteratur, Düsseldorf: Diederichs, 1978.

Meyer, J.E., (Death and Neurosis) *Tod und Neurose,* Göttingen: Vandenhoeck und Ruprecht, 1973.

Meyer, J.E., (Fear of Death and Consciousness of Death in Our Time) *Todesangst und das Todesbewußtsein der Gegenwart,* Berlin: Spring, 1979.

Mitscherlich, A. and M., (The Inability to Mourn) *Die Unfähigkeit zu Trauern,* Munich: Piper, 1967.

Parkes, C.M., Benjamin, B., Fitzgerald, R.G., "Broken Heart: A Statistical Study of Increased Mortality Among Widowers," *British Medical Journal,* 1, 1969, pp. 740-743.

Parkes, C.M., (Bereavement. Studies of Grief in Adult Life) *Vereinsamung, Die Lebenskrise bei Partnerverlust,* Hamburg: Rowohlt, 1978.

Pincus, L., (Until Death Do You Part, On the Psychology of Mourning) *Bis dass der Tod euch scheidet, Zur Psychologie des Trauerns,* Stuttgart: Deutsche Verlagsanstalt, 1977.

Rank, O., *Beyond Psychology,* New York: Dover Publications, 1958.

Rilke, R.M., (Works) *Werke in 3 Bänden,* Frankfurt: Insel Verlag, 1966.

Rogers, C.R., "Towards a Theory of Creativity," in: H. Anderson (ed.) *Creativity and its Cultivation,* New York: McGraw Hill, 1959.

Scheler, M., (Death and Continuation, Collected Works, Vol. 10, Works from the Legacy) *Tod und Fortleben,* Ges. Werke, Bd. 10, Schriften aus dem Nachlass, Bd. 1, Bern, 1957.

Scherer, G., (The Problem of Death in Philosophy) *Das Problem des Todes in der Philosophie,* Darmstadt: Wissenschaftliche Buchgesellschaft, 1979.

Schmiedbauer, W., (The Helpless Helper) *Die hilflosen Helfer,* Hamburg: Rowohlt, 1977.

Schultz, H.J. (ed.), (Loneliness) *Einsamkeit,* Stuttgart: Kreuz Verlag, 1980.

Schwartländer, J. (ed.), (The Individual and His Death) *Der Mensch und sein Tod,* Göttingen: Vandenhoeck und Ruprecht, 1976.

Steinmeyer, L.M. (Depression) *Depression,* Stuttgart: Kohlhammer, 1980.

Szonn, G., (The Mourning Process Assisted by Katathymic Image Association) "Trauerarbeit mit dem Katathymen Bilderleben," in: H. Leuner (ed.), *Katathymes Bilderleben,* Bern/Stuttgart: Huber, 1980.

Volkan, V., "Typical Findings in Pathological Grief," *Psychiatric Quarterly,* 44, 1970, pp. 231-250.

Volkan, V., "A Study of a Patient's 'Re-grief Work.' " *Psychiatric Quarterly,* 45/1, 1971, pp. 255-273.

Weischedel, W., (Sceptical Ethics) *Skeptische Ethik,* Frankfurt: Suhrkamp, 1980.

Wilhelm, R. (ed.), (I Ching – The Book of Changes) *I Ging – Das Buch der Wandlungen,* Düsseldorf: Diederichs, 1970.

Wilke, H.J., (Authority Complex and Authoritarian Personality Structure) "Autoritätskomplex und authoritäre Persönlichkeitsstruktur," *Analytische Psychologie,* 8, 1977, pp. 33-40.

Willi, J., (The Pair Relationship) *Die Zweierbeziehung,* Hamburg: Rowohlt, 1975.

Williams, M., "The Fear of Death," *Journal of Analytical Psychology,* 3, 1958, pp. 157-165.

Wiplinger, F., (The Individual Meaning of Death) *Der Personal Verstandene Tod,* Freiburg: Alber, 1980.

Wittkowski, J., (Death and Dying, Results of Thanato-psychology) *Tod und Sterben, Ergebnisse der Thanatopsychologie,* Heidelberg: Quelle und Meyer, 1978.

McGlashan, Alan
The Savage and Beautiful Country

Alan McGlashan presents a sensitive view of the modern world and of time, of our memories and forgetfulnesses, joys and sorrows. He takes the reader on a safari into regions that are strange and yet familiar: into the savage and beautiful country of the mind.

ISBN 3-85630-517-3

Talking with Angels
transcribed by Gitta Mallasz

The true story of four young artists who encountered wise and helpful spiritual forces in Nazi-occupied Hungary. These 'angels' gave them strength and a message of hope for the world.

ISBN 3-85630-505-X

ENGLISH PUBLICATIONS BY **DAIMON**

The Savage and Beautiful Country, Alan McGlashan
A Testament to the Wilderness, Ed. by R. Hinshaw
Talking with Angels, (transcribed by Gitta Mallasz)
A Time to Mourn, Verena Kast
Imprints of the Future, George Czuczka
Healing Dream and Ritual, C.A. Meier
Meetings with Jung, E.A. Bennet
Life Paints its own Span, Susan Bach
The Myth of Meaning, Aniela Jaffé
Was C.G. Jung a Mystic? Aniela Jaffé
From the Life and Work of C. G. Jung, Aniela Jaffé
Friedrich Nietzsche, Liliane Frey-Rohn

Jungian Congress Papers:

Jerusalem 1983: *Symbolic and Clinical Approaches*
Ed. by Luigi Zoja, R. Hinshaw

Berlin 1986: *The Archetype of Shadow in a Split World*
Ed. by M.-A. Mattoon

Available from your bookstore or from our distributors:

All territories
Daimon Verlag
Am Klosterplatz
CH-8840 Einsiedeln
Switzerland
Tel. (55) 53 22 66

Great Britain
Element Books Ltd.
Longmead Shaftesbury
Dorset SP7 8PL
England
Tel. (0747) 51 339

U.S.A.
Sigo Press
25 New Chardon St. # 8748
Boston, MA 02114
Tel. (617) 523-2321

U.S.A. West
The Great Tradition
750 Adrian Way,
Suite 111
San Rafael, CA 94903
Tel. (415) 492 9382